Dr. Baedeker

F. W. Baedeker, Ph.D.

DR. BAEDEKER
AND HIS
APOSTOLIC WORK IN
RUSSIA

by

Robert Sloan Latimer

With Introductory Notes by
Her Highness Princess Nathalie Lieven
of St. Petersburg
and
The Right Honourable Lord Radstock

SCRIPTURE TESTIMONY EDITION

WALKING TOGETHER PRESS
ESTES PARK · JENTA MANGORO

Published in 2023 by
Walking Together Press
Estes Park, Colorado USA
Jenta Mangoro, Jos, Plateau Nigeria
https://walkingtogether.press

ISBN: 978-1-961568-08-2

Dr. Baedeker and His Apostolic Work in Russia is in the public domain
Originally published in 1907 by Morgan & Scott, London

Cover design by D. Thaine Norris
Typeset in Adobe Garamond Pro by Lengdung Tungchamma and D. Thaine Norris

1

About the Scripture Testimony Edition

D_{R.} FREDERICK BAEDEKER, born in Germany in 1823, earned a doctorate in philosophy, became a successful business man and educator, then founded a high-class school in Weston-super-Mare, England, to where he emigrated, married, and settled into a prosperous life. But at age forty-three, Baedeker attended a series of evangelistic meetings about which he said, "I went in a proud German infidel, and came out a humble, believing disciple of the Lord Jesus Christ."

Through aristocratic connections, God granted Dr. Baedeker unprecedented access to the horrible prisons of Czarist Russia. Instead of enjoying the comforts of his upper-class position, he chose to spend his days and his wealth to visit the downcast and forgotten so that he might lift their chins with the hope of the glorious Gospel. Frequently in great need, or danger, or facing opposition, Dr. Baedeker sought and found deliverance through prayer. These proofs of God's love and faithfulness are chronicled in story after story in this powerful biography.

The Scripture Testimony Index is an extensive research project by Walking Together Press to use artificial intelligence and data science to develop a New-Testament-driven subject index across a large body of missionary biographies and personal narratives. In analyzing the database of these books programmatically; beautiful, bright threads emerge, threads of prayer, provision, deliverance, specific leading, healing, transformation, and miraculous salvation. The end result is an index of short story excerpts organized by subject and Scripture verse that empirically demonstrate the truth of the Scriptures, and which is freely available on our website at https://walkingtogether.life.

Walking Together Press has enhanced this classic title, *Dr. Baedeker and His Apostolic Work In Russia,* by identifying and marking thirty portions of the narrative that illustrate specific Biblical topics and verses. A *Scripture Testimony Index* has also been added containing short summaries of how each Scriptural topic is illustrated, making locating specific stories easy. Furthermore, this title is one of many in the *Scripture Testimony Collection.*

This Volume
Is Affectionately Dedicated to

Mrs. Baedeker

Who, for Fourty-four Years was the Loyal Help-meet of the Man
of God whose Life-story is herin sketched; and who, by her
Like-mindedness, her Loving Co-operation, her Generous
Financial Assistance in his many Projects, her
Willing Surrender of him to Urgent Calls
of Service, and her Patient Endurance
of the Anxieties of his Frequent and
Protracted Abscences from Home,
made such a Life-Adventure
for Christ possible.

With a swift rush the intolerable craving
    Shivers throughout me like a trumpet call,
Oh to save these, to perish for their saving,
    Die for their life, be offered for them all!
                        F. W. H. Myers, "St. Paul."

Preface

THIS book has been written to the glory of God. A life-work so signally exemplary in its long-sustained heroism for Christ, and so rich in spiritual stimulus, could not be allowed to pass unchronicled.

How great has been my privilege in being permitted to write it! It has been a means of grace to my own soul. I have transcribed many sentences from the doctor's letters and diaries with deepest emotion. He shows us his heart so artlessly and so fully; and it is so utterly possessed by his Lord!

It must be borne in mind that here are but a few fragments of the story of this extraordinary man.

Grateful thanks are accorded to Miss EDITH JONES and Mr. DOUGLAS RUSSELL, also to Messrs. R. E. SPARKS, B.A., and W. H. BENNET, Editors of *Echoes of Service,* for useful material kindly placed at my disposal.

R. S. LATIMER.

BRIXTON,

    LONDON, S.W.

Contents

List of Illustrations

Introductory Note

by Her Highness
Princess Nathalie Lieven
of St. Petersburg

THE late Dr. F. W. Baedeker was a frequent and ever-welcome guest in our home. Many of his meetings, as well as those of George Müller, were held in my house. I regard it as a great privilege granted to me by my Heavenly Father, to have been permitted to show hospitality to such eminent Christians.

We are deeply thankful to our Lord for having sent His faithful servant, Dr. Baedeker, to Russia. He was much loved there. The simple brethren called him "dedouchka" (dear grandfather). Love to his Lord and Master ever filled his heart. Often we heard him singing with all his heart the following hymn—

"What can wash away my stain?
Nothing, but the blood of Jesus!
Nothing, but the blood of Jesus!"

That this biography may be a great blessing to all who read it, for our Lord's glory, is the sincere wish of

Yours, in the Coming Lord,

N. LIEVEN.

St. Petersburg.

Introductory Note

by the Right Honourable Lord Radstock

IN common with thousands of others, I thank the Lord for His grace as seen in dear Baedeker. From the day when he came to the Lord in 1866, to the day of his home-call, he was a lovely witness for Christ. As soon as the glorious news came to him he began to make it known to others; and when his own professional work was done, spite of very feeble health, he visited the neighbouring villages to spread the glad tidings. Though so feeble that he sometimes even fainted on the way, he pushed on "faint yet pursuing."

His first Christmas holidays he spent in Bethnal Green, London, serving his Lord among the poorest

His labours "in journeys oft," especially crossing Siberia, often galloping in carts without springs, with a weak heart and delicate spine and lungs, were an example of the "faith that worketh by love." And he did not trust in vain. Starting on long and arduous journeys which to the natural eye seemed utterly beyond *his* strength, yet "his bow abode in strength." It was true of him, "this one thing I do," I press forward toward the mark.

The quondam unbeliever was a glorious instance of the child-like, dauntless life of faith.

Many hundreds of suffering Stundists, and tens of thousands of others, in Russia, Germany, Switzerland, and other lands, will call him blessed, for he trusted and glorified the Blessed One!

RADSTOCK.

4 Park Square, London, N.W.

Dr. Baedeker

CHAPTER I

A Man sent from God

GOD gave us some great saints in the end of the nineteenth century; men whose utterances, character, and good deeds greatly advanced and enriched the spiritual life of Christendom. In the roll of these illustrious sons and prophets of God is the name of Frederick William Baedeker. He came to England in 1859, and has resided here since that year, unknown even by name to the great majority of the citizens of the country of his adoption. Since his conversion in the year 1866, he has lived the life of a wanderer in foreign lands; making but occasional and brief visits to his home in our island, as Elijah retired to the solitudes of Horeb.

There was indeed something of a likeness between Baedeker and Elijah. Both appear to the public view in the simple dignity of a manhood fully equipped for high and urgent service. Neither has left any writings for future generations to study, therein seeking what manner of man the author had been. Both were enthusiasts, of inflexible will and vast ambitions for God; who, leaving to men of lesser soul, narrower spheres, and puny achievements, "thought in continents," and undertook great adventure for humanity and the kingdom of God.

On the other hand, while we are accustomed to think of Elijah as a stern prophet, of severe mien, who was not averse to the coercive method on occasion, Dr. Baedeker was among the meekest and most lovable of mortals; in his own person a veritable presentation of his Master's most persuasive and gracious invitations.

> **SCRIPTURE TESTIMONY**
>
> *Faith and love are demonstrated by giving of oneself for others*
>
> I JOHN 3:16-18

Mr. R. C. Morgan has faithfully sketched the man in the following sentence: "Many a lonely man and woman ceased to be friendless from the moment Dr. Baedeker Crossed their path. The prominent feature of his character was so essentially love, that we could never look at him without this thought flitting across our mind, 'So must the Apostle John have looked when he was aged.'"

Those who were privileged to know him at all intimately will bear, witness to the accuracy of this description. His extravagance in travelling rugs reveals the man. He seldom left England without being the proud possessor of a thick, warm, new rug—the gift of his wife—to fold about him. He seldom returned to England with that rug in his possession!

"Where is your rug? What have you done with it?" inquired his faithful spouse.

"Let me see! Ah, yes! There was a poor, shivering creature travelling on the deck of a Black Sea steamer, I wrapped it around her shoulders!"

The doctor was the contemporary and the friend of George Müller, of Bristol. The two men had much in common. Both were of German birth. In the land of their adoption they were near neighbours. They held similar views of truth. They both looked up into the face of the Heavenly Father with the artless faith of little children. Very humbly and very sincerely they both asked, "Lord, what wilt Thou have me to do?" And, each receiving his special answer, they both set about the appointed duty, spending themselves to the last ounce of their physical energy and to the last thought of their mind, in the Lord's service. Both were spared to reach a ripe and beautiful old age, far beyond the threescore years and ten. And both were permitted to serve to the very end of life in the spheres they loved so well.

George Müller brought to England those methods of practical Christian philanthropy he had learned in Germany, from the labours, among needy children, of Professor Franke in Hallé. Dr. Baedeker took back to the Continent that message of simple evangelical religion he had learned at the feet of Earl Cavan and Lord Radstock in England. Thus Bristol and Britain have been enriched by the magnificent object-lesson in Christly pity imported from Europe, and Europe has been vastly blessed—particularly Russia—by the Divine Gospel of faith, hope, love, and eternal life, exported from England.

In personal appearance Dr. Baedeker fulfilled the ideal of one of the great Hebrew prophets. A tall, spare figure, with long and venerable beard, the old man faced his audiences with the Divine fire in his eyes, as one illumined from Heaven and sent on a mission that would brook no delay.

He lived in the perpetual sunshine. His smiling face and cheery greeting brought you into the sunshine too. If, in bidding him "Good-morning," you inquired after his health, his answer would be, with a merry laugh, "God is good!"

The Christian faith is judged by the evidences it is able to produce. There are no more effective pieces of evidence than the lives of the saints. Then the life-story of this man of God ought to be familiar everywhere. Here is indeed noble consecration. Next to the Word of God, I cannot imagine a surer fountain of inspiration to the young manhood of our times, than is to be found in such a character and such a career as his.

When we consider him, not as a mere exponent of tricks of rhetoric or the arts of eloquence—these he disregarded; nor as the favourite idol of a clamorous and not always discriminating popularity—he was never that; but rather, in the vastness of the range of his ministry, the extreme variety of its spheres; the intensity and directness of its character, and the profound impression created by it, Dr. Baedeker was unquestionably one of the greatest evangelical preachers of this, or any age.

CHAPTER II

His Mission and His "Parish"

FROM the banks of the Rhine, in the neighbourhood of which he was born, to the last desperate penal settlement of Saghalien, beyond the Gulf of Tartary in farthest Asia; and from the princely homes of devout nobles in Stockholm, to the rough and bare settlements of Stundist exiles in the Caucasus at the foot of Mount Ararat, roved this apostle of two continents.

Up and down Europe; away over Siberia; to and fro by rail and by boat; by droshky or tarantass along interminable roads and tracks; by sledge across the wide snows of the steppes and along the course of frozen rivers; hither and thither this extraordinary man journeyed, preaching the gospel. Indeed the horseback exploits of John Wesley in evangelising England are completely dwarfed by the side of these thousands upon thousands of miles of travel undertaken by Dr. Baedeker ceaselessly, these many years in the service of Christ.

For what purpose? To preach and win sinners to repentance. To circulate diligently the Word of God in many languages, and thus scatter the seed of the Kingdom in expectation of a golden harvest. And chiefly, to hearten and help the children of God who were far removed from all Christian fellowship. To confirm these disciples in their faith; to be the sanctified vessel of gold "meet for the Master's use," in His "great house"; to be the instrument of the Holy Ghost the Comforter to multitudes of scattered, lonely, persecuted, outcast saints; to take to them the inexpressible joy, refreshment, and exhilaration that come from contact with a kindred human soul, from the warm pressure of a brother's hand, from the glance of sympathetic and affectionate human eyes, this was perhaps the most characteristic feature of his lifework. In it he laboured untiringly for many years. He thought nothing of himself. He cared little for fatigue or perils or long-continued privation. His charming home in Weston-super-Mare wooed him in vain from the snow-covered steppe, and the wolf-haunted mountain, and the miseries of travel in out-of-the-way and semi-civilised region?

Called of God in the prime of his manhood, he sternly refused the temptation to ease and luxurious indolence, and laid his splendid gifts of culture and of utterance upon the altar of Christ with whole-souled enthusiasm, dedicating his life to arduous evangelistic labours.

With the great Apostle of the Gentiles he could say: "In journeyings often, in labours more abundant, in prisons more frequent, in perils of waters, of robbers, by mine own countrymen, by the heathen, in the city, in the wilderness." At the advanced age of eighty-three years he laid down his service and passed into his Master's presence; but even in his last year upon earth he paid no fewer than four visits to the Continent in the interests of struggling communities of Christians there, who stood in need of his counsels and his aid. For him there came ho period of rest, until he entered into the rest of his Father's house.

Said one who knew him intimately: "He was quite indifferent as to what might happen to him. His life was of no importance whatever, except as he might lay it out for God. To lay it out, or to lay it down, it mattered not which, so long as God was glorified."

Those singular people, the Molokans—the Quakers of Russia—held a warm place in his affections. He had laboured amongst them, and admired their fearless adhesion to their anti-military principles, which occasioned them much suffering and privation in that great military state.

Sometimes in the largest room in the castle of an awakened Austrian nobleman who had called together his neighbours to hear his evangelist-guest; at other times in the quadrangle of an Armenian orphanage in Constantinople; now, in Smyrna, among a medley of Greeks, Armenians, Turks, and Jews, delivering six addresses in one day to people feverishly eager to hear the Word; then, in the class-room of a Hungarian, or Finn, or Russian University, to an assembly of theological students, while one of their own professors translated the address into their language; and again, in Munich among the. German socialists—his own fellow-countrymen—in the very hall where Karl Marx delivered his socialistic lectures, this busy apostle of Christ crowded a dozen lives into one in the multiplicity of his toils for the souls of men. What interesting and even thrilling experiences he related on his visits to his home and to his Christian friends in England! Everywhere he found the harvest ripe for the reaping, the people eagerly, and with deep emotion, receiving the Word.

For many years his face was quite familiar in every large city, and in many of the towns and villages of Central and Eastern Europe; and people joyfully recognised him wherever he went, as an old friend. In most places he had, among the residents, beloved friends who were proud to demonstrate their affection for "dear father Baedeker," by helping with his arrangements for meetings, etc.

A cousin of the "Baedeker" of Continental Guide-Book renown, and a contributor to several of his valuable Guides, particularly those referring to remote and out-of-the-way places, the doctor has been a guide to untold thousands in their journey to the Heavenly City.

The letters he received from abroad! There passed under his eyes during those consecrated years a continual stream of facts that might have been woven into a library of volumes of thrilling interest. One—a type of many— is from a Christian wife and mother in Transcaucasia, whose husband—a Stundist—has been in transportation eight and a half weary years for the crime of faithfulness to his Lord. What a tragedy, the story of that home!. And yet what a thrill of pride and joy in the lost husband-hero breathes in the lonely woman's simple narrative! Another is from the anxious pastor of a little church of believers in Saxony, who seeks guidance from his "beloved father" in a position of perplexity. A third is from a countess whose estates lie near the banks of the Danube, who says in modem language, "Come over into Macedonia and help us. You must not forget us, dear Dr. Baedeker; Austria greatly needs you. You *must* come, and come quickly." A fourth is from one whose eyes are watching for the morning of a brighter day, in Tiflis and who replies to Dr. Baedeker's advice that he should emigrate to a land of wider liberties: "Why should we emigrate? Do we not pray to God that He will give us freedom to serve Him here, in our own dear native country? We therefore expect that He will answer us!"

The Russian Armenians of the Caucasus, the Turkish Armenian refugees, and the orphan children of the victims of Turkish blood-thirstiness; the Stundists whom he contrived to meet secretly, in lonely places, in the dead of night, by hurried appointment, that he might convey to them the messages and love-gifts of their fellow-believers in Britain; the Mennonite Baptists, descendants of the sober, industrious colonists whom the Empress Catherine welcomed to her dominions a hundred years ago, and who, like their fathers, delight greatly in the Word of God; the newly illuminated Protestants of Austro-Hungary, whose motto is, "Free from Rome," and many of whom are so desirous, in the freshness of their freedom, to learn the pure gospel truth; these, and many other peoples, all most interesting, were included in the diocese of this catholic and apostolic bishop of the Church of God.

The name of Dr. Baedeker is cherished in many thousands of homes to-day throughout the world, with veneration; and it will be handed down to generations yet unborn as the name of a great-souled saint, who came from a far foreign shore, for love of souls and for love of Christ, to guide many stumbling feet into the way of peace.

The Rev. W, Blake Atkinson, formerly rector of Bradley, Worcestershire, has written the following beautiful lines in memory of the doctor. He kindly permits me to reprint them.

"He travelled wide, he journeyed far,
Where tyranny and darkness are:
And in his hand he bore God's Book,
And on his face he wore the look
Which only shines from those that show
The light of Heaven's reflected glow.

"And wheresoe'er he went, God's grace
Illumined every gloomy place:
And men, enthralled unjustly there,
A freedom found divinely fair;
While souls, long sunk in sin and crime,
Heard of redemption's plan sublime.

"O man of God! we will not scan
The narrow bounds of Church or clan.
We only know that men like thee
Are noblest of earth's chivalry,
And blazon forth, all ranks above,
The truth Divine that 'God is love.'"

CHAPTER III

Early Years

THERE lived at Witten, in Westphalia, in the early years of the nineteenth century, a clever naturalist named F. W. J. Baedeker, and his wife Frederika. To them were born six children, four boys and two girls. Dr. Baedeker, born on the 3rd August 1823, was their youngest son but one.

Mr. Baedeker the elder was an expert ornithologist, particularly learned in all that pertained to oology. He possessed a valuable collection of birds and their eggs, which included many rare specimens. After his decease these treasures were deposited in a natural history museum in Berlin. He also published an elaborate and beautifully illustrated work on *The Eggs of European Birds;* the numerous planes of which were prepared from illustrations painted by his own hand from the original specimens in his possession. There are eggs of all sorts and sizes, of "every bird of every wing," from those of the eagle and the stork, down to those of the different species of the little hedge-wren; eggs of many shades of colour, blue, brown, and green; eggs of pearly whiteness, and eggs speckled. A fascinating work it is, to the lover of nature. So wide was its author's fame that, from remote parts of Europe eggs of rare wild-fowl were sent to him for identification.

The naturalist was evidently an upright and conscientious man, if not devout; for we read in his son's diary of earnest conversations, between parent and child, in which young Fritz was faithfully and tenderly exhorted to eschew the evil and cleave to the good.

Fritz was a delicate and sensitive lad, who appreciated intensely little kindnesses from those around him. His mother appears to have been somewhat of a Spartan. Perhaps her four clamorous sons and her studious detached husband rendered it the more necessary that she should develop and display the sterner side of her character. Fritz turned to his elder sister Pauline for sympathy and affection; and Pauline gave them to him in unstinted measure.

At the age of sixteen, Fritz was apprenticed for three years to a business firm in Dortmund, and at twenty-one he entered the German army for his two years of military service. His regiment was stationed at Cologne, and his military experience was enlivened by the visit of Queen Victoria and Prince Albert to Germany. There were of course, grand decorations, brilliant illuminations, and many demonstrations of popular good will in the streets and squares of Cologne, when Her Majesty and the Prince entered the city.

In 1848 young Baedeker was again called upon by the authorities to leave business and join the Reserve. While engaged in his military duties his health broke down, and he was sent to the hospital. As there appeared to be no prospect of a permanent improvement, he received with joy his discharge from the Army.

His first marriage took place in 1851 to Auguste Jacobi; but the married life, begun in June, ended in September, when his young bride died.

Then his wanderings began, first to different parts of Germany, and afterwards (in 1854) to London, whence he sailed by the French barque *Banca* to Launceston, Tasmania. During the voyage the ship encountered a violent gale, and the crew found it needful to make desperate efforts against great odds, in order to save the vessel and the lives of those on board. However, in the mercy of God they, weathered the storm; but the voyage lasted over one hundred and thirty days!

In Launceston the young adventurer engaged himself as a tutor in French and German, first in a private school, and afterwards at Christ College; After two years here, he left for Melbourne, and later, sailed in a schooner to Sydney.

Two years were spent roving hither and thither in Australia; and in 1858 he returned to Europe in a French sailing ship bound for Havre, *viâ* Cape Horn. He was ninety days on the voyage. From Havre, Baedeker went by river-steamer up the Seine to Paris; and after spending a short time in that city, he crossed the frontier and gave a pleasant surprise to his parents and brothers and sister (Pauline had died during his absence), by appearing once again under the parental roof.

In the next year (1859) Baedeker came for the second time to England to visit some friends at Canterbury, whose acquaintance he had made in his travels. With one of them he visited Weston-super-Mare; and being invited by a gentleman named Girdlestone to join him in opening a high-class school in this town, he decided to bring to an end his unsettled life, and become a staid British citizen.

Among his first pupils was a lad named Harry Ormsby, whose mother was the young widow of Captain Ormsby, of the British Navy in Indian waters, and sister of the late Archdeacon Leigh-Lye of Bombay. To this lady Mr. Baedeker was happily married on 17th June 1862.

The conversion and consecration to the service of the Lord Jesus, of Dr. and Mrs. Baedeker are related in the following chapter. It may be well to add, that a few years later, Dr. Baedeker and his wife removed to Bristol, in order that he might attend certain lectures on medicine and surgery in connection with a hospital in that city. These studies he continued for about twelve months; and the knowledge thus acquired was of great service to him in his subsequent career. He was also, during his residence in Bristol, brought into intimate association with George

Müller, and the foundations of a close and valued friendship were laid, that lasted until the death of Müller. His degree in Philosophy was gained in the University of Freiburg. The doctor also studied at Bonn University, while residing in Germany.

It is interesting to find that one of the scenes of his earliest evangelistic labours was Witten, his birthplace and the home of his youth. To the man that was healed, the Master said, "Go home to thy friends, and tell them how great things the Lord hath done unto thee."

This brief chapter may fittingly close with extracts from three letters from Witten.

"'A prophet in his own country.' The verse applies to me here in its full meaning. Yet I trust the Lord will not fail to give me what I need, and what He requires for the people here. There is a praying band, and that comforts me."

"I have great joy in fellowship with Pastor Koenig, and Pastor Kellermann, whose wife is a daughter of my cousin. You would have been glad if you could have seen so many of my old school-fellows coming up to me, holding out their hands to me, and thanking me. We had a solemn time, praise the Lord!

"To-day I go to Annen, for a meeting in a hall belonging to the church, under the auspices of the clergyman."

"I called this afternoon on some distant connections of mine. They are strong Lutherans....

"Hitherto the Lord has prepared the way, and prospered me. On Wednesday I held a meeting in Annen. There is a *living* pastor there also. I walked back to Witten after the meeting, several friends accompanying me.

"The doctrine of Baptismal Regeneration is the shroud in which lies the corpse of the religious life of Germany. But the Spirit of God is at work among the people."

Mrs. Baedeker
Photograph by Mr. T. J. Kerslake

CHAPTER IV

His Conversion and setting forth for Christ

DR. BAEDEKER'S conversion took place at one of a series of meetings arranged by the late Earl of Cavan, and conducted by Lord Radstock, at Weston-super-Mare, in the year 1866. Under the preaching of that consecrated nobleman a great outpouring of the Spirit of God was witnessed in the town and neighbourhood. Many notable conversions took place. The influence of those times of Divine visitation is felt even to this day.

Mr. Douglas Russell has so vividly described the scene that we cannot do better than reproduce his words: "Through the importunity of a gentleman (himself a fruit of the work) of whom he had some acquaintance, Dr. Baedeker reluctantly consented to attend one meeting. Interest was awakened sufficiently for him to repeat his visit, but he was careful to make his exit before the noble preacher could reach him at the closing of the service. Having attended several meetings, the doctor one evening lingered long

<table>
<tr><td align="center">SCRIPTURE TESTIMONY</td></tr>
<tr><td align="center">Salvation transforms</td></tr>
<tr><td align="center">2 CORINTHIANS 5:16-
17 · GALATIANS 6:15</td></tr>
</table>

enough, or got far enough in without the ability to get out faster than the press would admit of, for Lord Radstock to reach him. Putting his hand on his shoulder, said he: 'My man, God has a message through me for you to-night,' urging him to enter the ante-room. In presence of the crowd he did so, and the two were soon on their knees. During those solemn moments a work was done in Dr. Baedeker whereby the accumulated infidelity of years was dissipated for ever. God was acknowledged, the Saviour trusted, and the joy of salvation soon filled his soul. The experience of that memorable night would be by himself thus tersely expressed: 'I went in a proud German infidel, and came out a humble, believing disciple of the Lord Jesus Christ. Praise God!'

"His wife, who had gone heart and soul with him into the world and its pleasures—music and dancing being their greatest delight—for some time stood aloof, and steered clear of

'These wondrous gath'rings day by day;'

but ultimately, seeing the change in her husband, and his determination to 'hold fast' and 'go forward,' said: 'Perhaps I am refusing something I ought to take,' accompanied him to a meeting, was awakened, and ere long, saved, and thus became a partaker of 'like precious faith.' 'As heirs together of the grace of life,' they were thenceforth one in purpose, constrained by the love of Christ who gave Himself for them, to spend and be spent for the best good of others."

And now a remarkable thing happened, A man who had for years been in delicate: health, who dare not even venture upon a walk with his wife without taking precautionary measures in case of heart failure, who was looked upon by all his acquaintances as foredoomed to an early grave, through feeble vitality, flung aside his medicine bottles, forgot that he suffered ominous pains, and stepped forth in the vigour of manhood's prime to serve Christ without an interval of serious illness for forty years.

Dr. Baedeker believed in his Lord for his body as well as for his soul. You never heard him complain of "feeling unwell" or even "weary." Christ bore his sicknesses as well as his sins. Of him it could be truly said, as of the subject of Apostolic healing, "His name, through faith in His name, hath made this man strong whom ye see and know; yea, the faith which is by Him hath given him this perfect soundness in the presence of you all," until his home-call at eighty-three years of age.

> **SCRIPTURE TESTIMONY**
>
> *According to your faith be it done to you*
>
> MATTHEW 9:27-31
>
> *There is healing in the name of Jesus*
>
> ACTS 3:6 · ACTS 3:16 · ACTS 4:10 · ACTS 4:30

Even on his dying bed he was far more concerned about the souls of his nurses than about his own bodily condition. If he could win two more jewels for Christ's crown it would be a fitting finish to his mortal career.

Lord Radstock was further privileged to open the "wide door and effectual" for Dr. Baedeker's ministry on the Continent. In the year 1874 his lordship paid a flying visit to Berlin; and in conference with some Christian friends in that city it was decided to send for a well-known American evangelist to conduct a mission there. Dr. Baedeker being then in the city, was requested to interpret for the foreign preacher. He interpreted with such spirit and power that the people said, "What need had we to send to America for a preacher? Here is a man of our own race and tongue upon whom the Holy Ghost manifestly rests. We will listen to him!"

Consequently, at the close of the tour throughout Germany with the American, the doctor struck out on independent lines, retracing the ground, revisiting the scenes of the recent meetings, and conducting with much blessing his first campaign for Christ in his own native country.

In the following year the doctor began his labours in Russia. To many persons of the highest social position in St. Petersburg he was introduced by his friend Lord Radstock, whose ministry has been attended with remarkable blessing in that Empire. In the year 1877, Dr. Baedeker let his house in Weston-super-Mare for three years, and with his wife and adopted daughter removed to Russia to resume his evangelistic labours primarily among the German-speaking populations of its towns and cities.

He subsequently extended his sphere far beyond the lines originally contemplated. Bohemia, Moravia, Hungary, Galicia, Poland, Switzerland, Finland, and the western and southern provinces of the vast Russian Empire have been the principal spheres of his ministry.

As soon as Dr. Baedeker began to preach, God began to bless. In the spring of 1875 he was conducting a mission in the Garrison Church, Berlin. A great many persons belonging to the aristocracy of the city were attracted, "and the power of the Lord was present to heal.' On 14th April the subject of his address was: "The way and work of the Holy Ghost in interpreting and applying the Sacrifice of Christ."A lady in the congregation, Fraulein Tony von Blücher, afterwards well-known throughout the Empire for her works of piety and charity, listened to that address with deep emotion. She went home, and retiring to her room "agonised to enter in at the strait gate."

"Now, Lord, or never!" was her cry.

<table>
<tr><td>SCRIPTURE TESTIMONY</td></tr>
</table>

God's work will not lack God's supply

PHILIPPIANS 4:19

God using an inner voice to communicate

ACTS 10:19-20 · ACTS 11:12

She rose from her knees a new creature in Christ Jesus, and began to work for the Lord immediately. She threw open her house for prayer-meetings and Bible-readings; went out into the highways of Berlin and gathered in her sisters and taught them the way of the Lord, and opened a Sunday school for children. Eight years afterwards she opened, on the anniversary of the day of her conversion, the "Saal am Schöneberger Ufer" for mission purposes. The building was soon too small. The friends held a meeting on Christmas Eve of that year to wait on the Lord respecting more accommodation and a larger hall. While they were in prayer the door opened, and a lady—a stranger—was announced.

"Last night," she said, "God laid upon my heart to bring you these two hundred marks to help you extend your work."

With this swift answer to their prayer the workers were greatly encouraged. The premises were enlarged, and rooms for the meetings of the various societies connected with the Central Mission were added. George Müller, Dr. Baedeker, and other beloved brethren from time to time conducted meetings there, and always with blessed results. There are in India and in China to-day missionaries at work for Christ who were brought to God at Fraulein von Blücher's mission. She received the home call in 1906. An interesting biography of her has been published in Berlin, from which the above brief particulars have been gleaned.

It was at Mitau, in Courland, that the doctor held his first meeting in Russia. From his hotel he made his way to the residence of the Governor.

"I am staying in your city for a few days. See, here is my passport. I am from England. I am an evangelist, and should like to hold a meeting here. If you will arrange for a meeting in your drawing-room, I am willing to conduct it, and deliver an address."

Imagine tackling an English mayor in this fashion! The worthy functionary would probably stagger into apoplexy. But gospel meetings are not so common in that land as with us.

"With the greatest of pleasure," replied the Governor; "My drawing-room is at your service, and my friends will be 'at your service' also. I will see that you have a large meeting."

In fulfilment of his promise he called his friends and his neighbours together, as did Cornelius the centurion of Caesarea, when Peter was expected on an identical errand, and no preacher could desire a more attentive or wistful audience than that which assembled to hear the Word in the state drawing-room of the Mitau "mansion-house."

On his arrival in a town or city, Dr. Baedeker usually made inquiry if there was an Evangelical Christian man in the place. If so, he would seek him out and consult him as to the next steps, the hire of a hall, notifying the numerous authorities, and so forth. If not, he almost invariably adopted the course he took at Mitau; and his request for a drawing-room meeting at the Governor's house was generally most graciously complied with. There was one serious drawback, the paintings on the walls.

The doctor, when at home in England, sometimes distressed his good wife by grumbling at the pictures on his own drawing-room walls. Mrs. Baedeker naturally saw nothing wrong with them, and was perplexed. His singular prejudice had been created by the pictures on walls of the rooms of Governors' houses in which he had held his meetings. They were usually numerous. The spacious walls were often covered from ceiling to floor, three rows of them, and many of the pictures beautiful works of art. How was it possible for a preacher so to fascinate the attention of his auditory as to keep the eyes from roving occasionally to the feast of beauty so invitingly spread around?

But notwithstanding the pictures, a great harvest followed the scattering everywhere of this gospel seed. In the early days the doctor was obliged to seek and to obtain the permission of no fewer than five independent authorities in each place he visited, before he could open a hall to hold a meeting: (1) The civic head of the town or city, (2) the chief of the police, (3) the head of the education office, (4) the ecclesiastical chief, and (5) the newspaper censor (to obtain leave to insert his advertisement).

Sometimes his reception by these men "dressed in a little brief authority" was the reverse of polite. If he had not been a foreigner of distinguished bearing, and backed up by influence in high quarters, he would almost invariably have been refused.

"Who are you—Radstock?"

"No; Dr. Baedeker from England."

"What do you want—'to preach,' you say!" "Yes."

"Have you been to the Governor?" "Yes."

"And to the priest?" "Yes."

"And to the"—(some other official)? "No."

"Then you must see him before you come to me."

An thus the evangelist was sent from pillar to post among the local authorities until he was weary, before he was permitted even to open negotiations for the hire of a hall or room for his mission. Not infrequently a more intimate acquaintance with the doctor caused a complete revulsion of feeling in his favour. One particularly harsh officer was so completely won over by the kindly tactfulness of the evangelist, that at the close of the meetings he accompanied him to the station and with the warmest demonstration of hearty affection bade him farewell. Perhaps the debtor and the erstwhile surly official have ere this met in heaven; a soul won by the unwearied patience and graciousness of manner of this "imitator of God."

Was it any wonder that he usually cut the gordian knot by asking the Governor to arrange a semi-private meeting in his house? These restrictions are now in great part removed: an advance in the direction of religious liberty for which Russia may well praise God. I think too, as the years passed, the doctor became more venturesome; for in later years he boasted that he used to act on the simple principle of never asking permission at the outset.

"Go on until they stop you! It saves time."

As a consequence he several times found himself in trouble. But so familiar was he with the interior of gaols, that he had no objection to endure the temporary inconvenience of imprisonment. He often said that if he had to go to prison, he would prefer to do so in Russia, rather than in England. He might then preach to his fellow-captives.

CHAPTER V

Russia Yesterday and To-morrow

IN the early seventies the Spirit of God visited in great power the upper classes of Society in Russia. One of the most prominent instruments of that remarkable visitation was Lord Radstock, whose preaching and personal dealing with individuals were blessed to the enlightening and ingathering of many souls.

Mrs. Edward Trotter, in her work *Undertones of the Nineteenth Century,* instances one, the case of Count Bobrinsky, Minister of the Interior, "a man immersed in affairs." A casual conversation with Lord Radstock "resulted in a flood of light such as arrested Paul on the Damascus road."

Shortly after the Revival came a time of severe testing to the young disciples of the Lord. Under the notorious Pobiedonostzeff, Procurator of the Holy Synod for the long period of about thirty years, liberty of conscience was denied to Christians in the Empire. Fines, confiscations imprisonments, exile, were remorselessly imposed upon any who dared to differ from the Czar's religion.

The story of Colonel Paschkoff throws a flood of light on the difficulties and perils of evangelisation in the country of the Czar in the old days. Colonel Paschkoff was an officer of the Imperial Guards, a nobleman of considerable wealth, who loved and served the Lord Jesus. He owned a mansion in St. Petersburg and broad estates in different parts of Russia, including some valuable copper mines at Undorf, on the confines of Siberia, where is also a huge fortress-prison visited often by the good doctor.

<table>
<tr><td align="center">SCRIPTURE TESTIMONY</td></tr>
<tr><td align="center">Individuals opposed
to the Gospel

ACTS 8:3 · ACTS 9:1-2

Believers suffer for Christ,
not common crime

I PETER 4:12-19</td></tr>
</table>

The Emperor Alexander III banished this devout soldier because he would persist in evangelising, by drawing-room meetings for prayer and Bible study, by tract distribution, and among his friends by the familiar and persuasive method known as "button-holing." While in exile he wrote to the Czar, requesting permission to return temporarily to St. Petersburg for the purpose of attending to his affairs.

Two letters from Dr. Baedeker lie before me; both from St. Petersburg.

"A letter from Colonel Paschkoff to the Emperor, asking permission to visit Russia to look after his estates, is to be laid before His Majesty. We are all praying that the answer may be such as to glorify God."

Three days later he wrote:

"Dear Paschkoff has permission to come to Russia for three months. We are hoping to hear to-day when he will arrive. There is great joy at the prospect of seeing him once more, as you may imagine."

His return was indeed a time of great rejoicing among the little company of believers. Who could be surprised that they often called at his residence? And presently the Czar heard whisperings of more prayers and Bible-readings! He sent for the Colonel.

"I hear you have resumed your old practices!" he said sternly.

"My friends have certainly called to greet me, and we have prayed and read the Word of God together!" meekly replied the officer.

Colonel Paschkoff

"Which you know I will not permit," said the Czar. "I will not suffer you to defy me. If I had thought you would have repeated your offences you would not have been allowed to return. Now go; and never set your foot upon Russian soil again!"

And thus this faithful and godly man was exiled for ever from his native land for Christ's sake, as were many others at that time, the salt of Russian Society, "by order of the Czar!"

This same Colonel Paschkoff was, prior to his banishment, a valuable friend to the Stundists scattered over southern Russia. On one occasion he conceived the idea of a convention of Stundist representatives, and proceeded to carry out his scheme at his own expense. He engaged a roomy hotel in St. Petersburg and invited the widely scattered bodies to send delegates to the capital city for a series of meetings; arranging to pay the fares of all too poor to defray their own expenses, and to entertain them free of charge during their stay. They came, to the number of about four hundred. The meetings, I believe, were held in a hall in the palace of the Princess Lieven. Tickets were issued to each person; Dr. and Mrs. Baedeker's tickets being Nos. 1 and 2 respectively. Although many of the delegates were simple peasants and workmen from remote provinces, quite unfamiliar with the ways of the aristocratic circles of the fashionable metropolis, they won golden opinions by their respectable appearance, and quiet, agreeable, and devout manners. For the most part, a spoon thrust into one of their long boot-legs, and a comb into the other, comprised their sole travelling equipment. If the outfit was scanty, it was selected with a view to utility! Day after day was spent in solemn happy meeting; sounds of prayer and praise, all too unfamiliar beneath palace roofs, ascending to heaven. One morning the palace gates stood open and the hall was ready, with host and hostess, the Baedekers, and other friends awaiting as usual their arrival, but no delegate appeared. The hours passed, but no belated provincial arrived; nor during the day, nor the next day. Colonel Paschkoff was perplexed, and many were the conjectures as to the secret of the sudden disappearance of the guests.

He made inquiries. His hotel was deserted; and no tidings could he hear of them in any direction.

On the day but one following, one member of the vanished company appeared upon the scene, and in scared tones told his story and solved the mystery. On leaving the hall they had been, every one, arrested by a large force of police that had lain in wait for them. In the fortress of St. Peter and St Paul, whither they had been taken, they were carefully searched, and separately interrogated as to whence they had come, their purpose in coming, who paid their charges, and their opinions on political and other matters. It was alleged by the examining officials that revolutionary papers had been discovered on some of their number. At this they laughed loudly.

"The only revolutionary document possessed or used by any of us," they replied, "is the Bible. We aim at no revolution other than that which the Cross of our Lord Jesus Christ effects!"

"Oh, I daresay you are all very good people," said the principal officer when they were reassembled, "but you have no lawful business in St. Petersburg; and therefore we are going to send you all back at once to your homes. You will be accompanied to the railway stations, and the police will see you each booked and placed in the train for your respective destinations. If any of you are again discovered in this city, you will be arrested and punished!"

He who returned to tell the story was adroit enough to ask at the station for a ticket for a town not far from St. Petersburg, to which he took an early opportunity to return, risking his liberty in so doing in order to let his generous friends know what had become of their guests.

Such was the civil and religious atmosphere of the land in which Dr. Baedeker elected to serve Christ, and endeavoured—not in vain—to push forward the frontiers of His Kingdom.

In his addresses in England, Dr. Baedeker dwelt on the problem that Russia presents to the itinerating evangelist. A land of many nationalities and many languages —leaving altogether out of account Asiatic Russia, which comprises two-thirds of the Empire—there are, in addition to the Russians proper, the Tartars, Armenians, Poles, Letts, Finns, and many others. There are also many Germans resident in the country.

The doctor preached in English, German, or French, as the occasion demanded; but although he was familiar with Russ, he was not sufficiently sure of it to use it in preaching, except under pressure of circumstances. He was generally able to find a brother in Christ to translate into Finn, Fris, Russ, Lett, Georgian, Armenian, Esthonian, or any other of the bewildering multiplicity of languages spoken within the Empire.

Occasionally he would keep two, three, and even five interpreters going at one time, translating into different languages, each surrounded by a crowd of persons who understood his speech, while perhaps a few who understood the language—German, or English—in which the doctor was preaching, were grouped around the central figure. Sometimes it was even more complicated, as in cases where it was necessary to employ two interpreters to get the gospel into the mind of an audience; the first, to translate say from German into Russian, and the second to translate from the Russian into the language of the hearers. It would be interesting if we could compare the addresses and see the modifications in the original message as it passed through its multi-translations.

"I like to preach by interpreter," he said on one occasion; "it gives me a rest."

In the autumn of 1901, Mr. and Mrs. R. C. Morgan accompanied Dr. Baedeker on a tour of two months duration, through the Caucasus, visiting the prisons and addressing some thousands of prisoners. The following vivid picture of their crossing of the frontier is from the pen of Mrs. Morgan:

"We pass swiftly through Germany, reaching at midnight the Austrian frontier. After two hours of waiting we continue our journey *viâ* Cracow and Lemberg. The day is grey, and the country flat and poor. At ten p.m. we arrive at Woloczyska in pouring rain. The wind is high and cold, but we are kept warm by the proceedings that follow.

"'Have your passports ready,' says the doctor.

"We give them up before passing into the Customs Hall, where confusion seems to reign. Our hand-baggage is opened and every bit of print seized. After a little while the books are returned. With several copies of *The Christian,* our Bible notes, and other papers in hand, the official is endeavouring to explain matters to us. We shake our heads at the strange sounds. He raises his voice, but the louder he speaks, the more we shake our heads, until Dr. Baedeker comes to our rescue.

"'If you are willing to pay 50 kopeks, your printed matter will be sent to the office of the censor at Odessa,' he says.

"By his advice we prefer sacrificing our property. At the other end of the hall a motley crowd gathers around an official, who, behind a counter, is returning the passports. Our name being one of the last ones, we encounter no difficulties in the revision of our registered luggage; and now, by means of our passports and small tickets to show that our hand-bags had been duly examined, we pass into the waiting-room, which is at the same time the restaurant. Bright, shining samovars greet our eyes and we enjoy the amber-coloured beverage, called czaj (tea). A formidable amount of luggage has been heaped up at the entrance to the platform, and as soon as the door opens, there is a scramble and a shouting, passengers calling out for the number of their 'najsilstchiks' (porters), each trying to squeeze through first. We climb with others over the luggage barrier, and, half-dazed, follow the stream. Somebody good-naturedly pushes us into a compartment. It is the doctor, who has kept all the time a sharp eye upon us.

"'But where are our bags?' we ask, bewildered.

"'Have no fear,' is his quiet reply. In a short while, indeed, all is settled and as our train passes out of the station we begin to realise that we have crossed the threshold of Russia."

As to the future of Russia from the point of view of the gospel, the doctor was on the whole optimistic. He loved the land and the people. There does not appear to be in all his correspondence a syllable depreciative of the central governing powers; except here and there an ardent protest against the policy of religious intolerance and harshness—a policy that now, we trust, is practically a thing of the past. He was far too busy with urgent spiritual concerns to give his time to political affairs. He was never a meddler.

Brighter days are dawning, thank God! Much has been accomplished in the emancipation and evangelisation of the nations since a certain ruler emphasised his policy of the extermination of non-conforming Christians by exclaiming, "I would rather be the king of a desolate land than rule over a pack of heretics!" Dr. Baedeker has taken a noble part in this glorious advance in the direction of liberty and truth. Who can tell to what extent the awakening in the-soul of the Russian people of a passion for freedom, and justice, and brotherhood, is due to the many years of patient evangelising, up and down the vast realm, of this unwearied enthusiast!

Great progress has been made within the last few years. Some events we greatly deplore; but in others we un-feignedly rejoice. Since the ukase of 1861, by which twenty-three millions of serfs were emancipated owing to the enlightened and noble *civil* policy of the Czar Alexander II, no greater step in the recognition of the rights of humanity has been taken than that of 1905, when the present Czar gave his subjects freedom in matters of religion. The people are beginning to realise what a boon they enjoy. Baron Uexküll wrote recently to a friend in England:

"We are still under the influence of the greatest religious event of Russian history—the edict of liberty of conscience of 1905. It is go new and beautiful for Russian Christians now to have freedom to worship God as our conscience teaches us. We hear from all parts of the Empire that persons are leaving the Greek Orthodox faith and becoming Evangelical Christians."

That there is yet abundant room for improvement in civil administration, the following telegram from Warsaw, through *Reuter*, dated 3rd February 1907, will be sufficient evidence:

"As all the prisons and fortresses are filled to overflowing with persons who have lain confined in them without trial for many months, the Governor-General has ordered a committee, composed of representatives of the judicature, army, and police, to examine the prisoners, and to release those who were arrested owing to the excessive zeal of the authorities."

As the warm and kindly finger of the spring loosens the avalanche along the steep crests of the northern Urals as her gentle breath causes the frozen rivers of Siberia to heave and press and burst their icy masses with explosions like thunder; so influences new and mighty are playing upon the populations of the vast Russian Empire; influences political and social, moral and spiritual. May He who, sitting upon the floods, stilleth the noise of the-waves and the tumult of the people, give all grace to the Czar and his advisers, and to all leaders of men at such a time as this!

CHAPTER VI

"I was in Prison and Ye came unto Me"

FOR eighteen years the doctor enjoyed the unique privilege of free access to every prison within the dominions of the Czar, from Warsaw to the transportation settlements on the island of Saghalien, and from the fortress-prisons of Caucasia in the south to the most northerly desolations of icy Siberia.

His permit set forth that he was "under special command to visit the prisons of Russia, and to supply the convicts with copies of the Holy Scriptures." The wording of the document gave him a kind of official status; and his liberty to approach the prisoners in whatever manner he thought best, appears to have been seldom called in question; so wonderfully did God open up the way for his consecrated service.

"My name," said he on one occasion, "has become in Russia and Siberia a kind of latch for prison gates. I have as much freedom to preach Christ within the prison walls as I should have in any street in London—and, indeed, more." It was his privilege and joy to hand a copy of the New Testament to innumerable convicts, political and other, and to accompany the gift with a few loving words of hope and help concerning Him who is the Friend of sinners. Here was a ministry to which this man of God gave himself with intense devotion. Happily we have the story preserved as it came from his own lips, of the manner in which this privilege came to be granted to him.

"Formerly I had no idea of the large part of the population of many countries that are kept as if they were wild beasts behind iron bars and with heavy chains upon them. Learning the facts in Russia, my heart's desire was, 'Oh that the prisons might be opened to me!' I ventured to express my desire to a lady of rank in St. Petersburg, and asked her whether it was possible. She shook her head sadly. But she did not forget my desire."

Here it may be intimated that the "lady of rank" was a highly esteemed Countess, who was a personal friend of the Empress (grandmother of the present Czar) and the wife of a well-known Ambassador. The Countess was one day shopping in St. Petersburg. The Count, her husband, stood at the shop door waiting for her.

"Here, quickly!" he exclaimed.

"What is it?" she inquired, hastening to the door.

"There is the very man you want; on the other side of the road!"

"Whom do you mean?"

"The Director of the Prisons Department. He is the man to speak to about that 'permit' you have been inquiring for."

"Run, then, and call him back!" cried the Countess.

The Count hastened after the Official, and returned to the shop with him.

"May I have the honour to oblige your ladyship?"

"I would like you to supply my friend Dr. Baedeker, an Englishman, with a 'permit' to visit prisons and see the prisoners, not of course for a political purpose, but to give them Bibles and do them good."

"Does your friend think he can reform them?"

"He thinks God can, through His Word, the Gospel."

"Indeed, that is so, madam! I will certainly see that he has the permission he requires."

Let us now resume the doctor's personal statement.

"The 'permit' reached me here in England, as I was about to start for Russia, and I looked upon it as a wonderful gift indeed. Hastening on the journey, I got at last to

---

SCRIPTURE TESTIMONY

The righteous innately have God's heart toward those in need

MATTHEW 25:31-46

Odessa, and one of my first visits was to the prison. I showed my document, and it was good; the prison doors were opened, and the officers were most kind and considerate, and helped me in every way. This was indeed a wonderful answer to prayer. Ah! you little know the enormous number of people in every land who are kept out of sight, and are never thought of by others."

A year or two afterwards he was privileged to meet the Director of Prisons in St. Petersburg. Here is his own account of the interview:

"We talked very freely on the defects and the needs of the Russian prisons. He is a God-fearing man, and he has at heart the welfare of the prisoners. He told me his plans; and he said, 'With God's help I mean to effect great changes within two years.' He encouraged me to go to East Siberia, and promised to send the boxes of scriptures to the different prisons, addressed to me, to be kept until I arrived. He much wishes that I should go to Saghalien also; and he also promised to give me full information about the various prisons. Praise God for this open door!

"I called on Madame K. and told her of some of the terrible scenes I had witnessed. She went to see the Empress, and spoke about this to her; and the question was asked whether the lady-in-waiting would not have me to call and tell about it all, perhaps in the hearing of the Empress. Pray that all may be for the glory of the Name of the Lord. I fear nothing will be done, for great people soon forget, and Madame K. is gone to Helsingfors."

This tribute to the Head of the Prisons Department should be borne in mind when we are sitting in judgment on the authorities. Doubtless many of the improvements in the details of Russian prison administration effected in the following years were the direct results of the humane and sympathetic suggestions of Dr. Baedeker.

We are travelling too fast, however, and must return to early experiences.

Armed with his newly acquired authority, the doctor journeyed from fortress to fortress carrying the good tidings of great joy to the most degraded and the most miserable classes in the Empire, and incidentally, in cases not a few, ministering untold succour and comfort to some who lay in the dungeons of the Czar for Christ's sake and the gospel's.

On one occasion he was visiting the prison at Tver, a city on the river Volga, to the north of Moscow, prominently in the public eye recently in consequence of the murder there of Count Ignatieff by a Social Revolutionary Agent. To a congregation of eight hundred convicts, each in chains, with head half-shaved and ready for transportation on the morrow afoot to far Siberia, he had tenderly preached the gospel. The rest of the day he had spent in visiting from cell to cell and in personal dealing with individual souls until six o'clock in the evening. On his arrival at the railway station, to his chagrin he discovered that the Moscow train had gone, and there was not another until two a.m. There was nothing for it but to possess his soul in patience. In the waiting-room, before a comfortable fire, like many another traveller, he slept the sleep of the just. He was awakened by the scream of the incoming train. Opening the door he found the platform crowded with people. In the crush and scramble to secure a seat, his pocket-book was stolen from him. It was a serious loss, because it contained his passport, English money to the value of £100 notes for a thousand roubles Russian money, and —most calamitous of all—his precious prisons-permit!

On his arrival in Moscow he sat down with a sorrowful heart and wrote the story Of the loss of his "permit" to his friend the Countess. She replied by telegraph:

"I am getting another order for you. But have you lost anything else— any money."

The doctor admitted that he had lost a considerable sum of money, and also his passport. The good Countess and her friends in St. Petersburg would not suffer Dr. Baedeker to be one kopek the poorer for his misfortune, and when the fresh permit arrived from headquarters he discovered to his great joy that it was expressed in terms that gave him wider liberties and greater privileges in his prison ministrations than the document he had lost!

Thus "God turned the curse into a blessing," as is His wont in response to the prayers of His children; for all who knew Dr. Baedeker will be quite certain that he made this circumstance, in common with every other interest of his life, a matter of prayer before God.

> **SCRIPTURE TESTIMONY**
>
> *God is able to bring good from any circumstances*
>
> ROMANS 8:28

The prisons-permit was renewed every two years; and such was the confidence of the authorities in the doctor, that with almost every renewal there were granted to him, unsolicited, still larger privileges in his work, a wider opening of the jealously guarded doors of access to the fortress-prisons and penal settlements, in order that he might be able, unhampered by restrictions and regulations, to the utmost possible extent to pursue his self-denying labours for the spiritual and eternal welfare of the convicts.

Not only to the prisoners, but also to the warders and other officials were his visits blessed.

"I was an officer in —— fortress," said a gentleman whom he casually met in Russia about two years ago. "When you were speaking to the convicts there, *you hit me!*"

In the prison at Kutais in Transcaucasia the poor fellows clamoured eagerly around him, asking something of him in an unknown tongue.

"What is it they are begging for?" he inquired of his interpreter. "Is it money, or tea, or what?"

"It is only that you will write your name on little slips of paper, or in their Testaments, that they may more readily remember it."

"But why do they want to remember my name? It doesn't matter who I am. I am simply a servant of Christ."

"They want to keep your name before them, in order that they may constantly pray for you, for your great love to them!"

The doctor looked into the faces of the great crowd of convicts who stood before him. Right in the soft expression of their eyes he saw that his interpreter had translated their message aright. They were already praying for him.

"God bless the dear fellows!" he exclaimed. "They want to pray for me, do they? Then truly God has heard my prayer for them! They shall have my name!"

And in hundreds of little books the doctor wrote his name in Russian characters, "Бедекеръ"; and surely never did the bestowal of an autograph afford so much happiness or evoke so many tears.

Tears were the rule and not the exception when Dr. Baedeker preached in the prisons. God opened hard hearts to him marvellously.

Dr. Baedeker had at the outset many formidable obstacles to over-come in his prison-visitations. Although the officials could not—in face of his permit—refuse him admittance, nor refuse to allow him to preach in the prisons, some of them gave him to understand pretty plainly that he was not wanted. As the years passed, and visit succeeded visit, this hostility thawed into geniality and hearty reception, until he became, in nearly every prison he visited, the eagerly looked for guest of the Governor, welcomed with affection and parted from with regret. The meekness, kindliness, Christlikeness of the man it was, that so completely disarmed opposition, and turned the sullen foe into a cordial friend. Among his early experiences he related how in one prison, when he asked that arrangements should be made for him to address the convicts, he was told that the Governor had given instructions that they should not be assembled.

"They must remain in their kameras."

"Then I will visit them in the kameras."

"This cannot be permitted."

"But I have authority to address them! If the Governor will not give me access to them, how can I do so?"

"The Governor has instructed us to open the kamera doors to a small extent. If you wish to address them, you can do so from the corridor. But they will not be allowed to leave, nor you to enter, the kamera."

The preacher, like a wise man, made the best of the situation, and preached the gospel to an invisible congregation, that listened behind the slightly opened kamera doors, the watchful warders keeping jealous guard.

Subsequent permits gave him the right of access to the kameras and other privileges, and personal interviews of a most affecting nature often took place with the prisoners.

Take another instance of official obstruction in the early days. The doctor thought it would be helpful if he underlined suitable verses in the Gospels he was about to circulate in a certain prison, after the fashion of the familiar Marked Testament. He therefore took the trouble to go through several hundred portions of the Scriptures, and with his own hand marked in red ink selected verses that told of the Divine pity and grace for sinners. It was of course a slow and fatiguing labour; but his love of souls and of Jesus made it a real joy. When he began his work of putting the books into the eager hands of the prisoners, he called the attention of the recipients to the red marks.

The jealous eye of a high prison officer was at once turned upon him.

"What are you giving to that man?"

"A New Testament."

"But what are these red signs?" he inquired severely, taking the book and glancing over the leaves.

"Only the underlining of special texts."

"But these crosses on the margin—we cannot allow these!"

"They are merely to direct the reader's attention to suitable passages. I want the books to be a help and a blessing to them."

"You mean well; but it is against the regulations! Warder, collect the books already given out!"

"Against what regulations? I am not aware that I have broken any rule."

"The books you are allowed to circulate are expressly limited to 'Bibles or Testaments without note or comment.'"

"And these portions are 'without note or comment.'"

"That is not so. You have added your own-notes and comments in these underscorings and crosses. Their meaning you have just told me, is that these particular verses are especially suitable to their case. That is your opinion—your 'note and comment,' conveyed in red ink within the book. Warder, gather them all up! We cannot allow them to be retained. It is contrary to regulations."

The good doctor was obliged to submit His marked portions were reserved for a more auspicious occasion, and other copies were substituted.

How the doctor was loved and clung to by some of the miserable prisoners as though he were an angel from heaven, we, who have heard him tell, can bear witness. In his English home, in one corner of the drawing-room, there stands an elaborately carved photo-frame in which is a cabinet photograph of himself. The frame was carved in far Siberia by one of the captives, and given to the doctor as a love-token, and memento of his long journeys and strenuous labours in their behalf. "The day shall declare" the results. We may be quite sure our beloved friend will "come again with rejoicing, bringing his sheaves with him."

CHAPTER VII

In the Camp of the Angel

"DID the doctor gener-ally carry weapons?" a friend asked of Mrs. Baedeker.

"What do you mean?" she inquired.

"A revolver, for instance, as a precaution of protection; or a dagger, to use in an emergency. He was continually brought into association with all sorts of people, and—you never know."

"He would not dream of carrying such things! I have never known him even speak of them, all the years of his journeys abroad."

"Do you mean to say he went forth absolutely defenceless?"

"By no means. *God was his defence!*"

It was so. He dwelt in the camp of the angel. "The angel of the Lord encampeth round about." He never came to any serious harm, anywhere. Perhaps his worst peril was from diseases. But he passed scathless into and through over-crowded prison hospitals, where

the stench of the most virulent pestilences that can afflict humanity polluted the atmosphere, and where the doctors themselves were
frequently prostrated.

Softly the wings of the omnipresent God folded about the soul and
the body of His servant. Every expression in the ninety-first Psalm
had a significance for him, and an explicit fulfilment in his person.
Travelling incessantly by night and by day on his mission of mercy,
often in wild and scantily populated regions, where wild beasts and
desperate men have their haunts, he was never injured nor molested.
His assurance that he was the subject of the protecting care of God,
made him hold his life lightly.

When his friends, of late years, remonstrated with him on his under-
taking such long journeys at his advanced age, he would reply: "If my
Heavenly Father should call me home from a railway carriage, or from
a steamer, or from an hotel, why should I mind? What does it matter?"

> **SCRIPTURE TESTIMONY**
>
> *As we serve Him, the Lord*
> *will be our defense*
>
> LUKE 10:19 · 2
> THESSALONIANS 3:1-3

The spirit of the man cannot
be better illustrated than by the
following. A Russian gentleman of high rank told him of
a certain district in the remote
dominions of the Czar, where
hardship and solitude had
rendered the unhappy exiles desperate, and turned them into demons.

"The country is beautiful; but the inhabitants add to the brutal
degradation of the local Asiatics, the fierce savagery of European criminals," said his informant. "They will without hesitation shoot down
a man merely for the sake of his clothes and the few coins he may
possess. Twice they levelled their arms at me, but God preserved me.
Their common saying is: 'It pays better to shoot a man than to shoot
a partridge. The partridge is worth but a few kopeks at the, most; but
a man has at least his clothes, and there may be money also!'"

"Tell me all about them," said Dr. Baedeker eagerly. "I mean to go
there. Those people terribly need the gospel!"

He, went, of course; accomplished his mission, and returned unharmed.

"In all my journeys through the country, by day and by night," said he, "I never once saw the face of man turned towards me with evil intent."

The sweetness of Dr. Baedeker's disposition, his imperturbability and readiness to see the best in everybody and everything, were doubtless of value in securing him against molestation. We never discover a trace of irritability, even under most aggravating conditions. Who would care to be awakened at one in the morning by a pair of rowdy ruffians in a railway carriage, making night hideous with their shouts and horseplay? If you were not provoked to active resentment—which would not be prudent, as these fellows carry bright weapons, and use them on occasion—at all events when you wrote home to your wife you would indulge in a growl, and so relieve your, suppressed indignation, would you not? This is how the doctor viewed the situation:

> "*Tiflis.*—The dear Tartars! I cannot help loving them, even in their wild rough attire. Two fine men, Tartars, travelled with me in the train from Baku, and at one o'clock in the night they began making music and melody, one on a kind of guitar, the other on a tambourine. They were all alive in their music; every nerve and fibre in harmony, the two men like one. They played wild melancholy tunes, which only a solitary desert life can call forth. It was wonderfully beautiful! And now and then one sang in thrilling tones. There was no set tune, but a wild melodious outburst. They seemed grateful for being taken notice of; and I could not but lift up my heart to the Lord that He might tune these wild hearts to sing His praise! There was something wonderfully sweet and attractive in these men. May God open the fountain of living water to the Tartars!"

It was never among brutalised criminals, nor yet among inhabitants of remote regions, but in haunts of learning and circles of culture, that the most bitter hostility to his work was met with.

<table>
<tr><td>SCRIPTURE TESTIMONY</td></tr>
<tr><td>Escape from pursuers

ACTS 9:23-25</td></tr>
</table>

Early in his career, as evangelist, he paid a visit to Zurich, in Switzerland. He rented a château on the hillside outside the city, where his wife and he decided to remain for a few months, while he visited the people and preached the gospel in the neighbourhood. The fact that there were at that time a considerable number of Russian refugees living in the city, attracted him thither.

His first public meeting was billed to be held in a large public hall, the subject announced being "The Bible." The doctor had only one theme: "Jesus Christ, and Him crucified," under whatever title it was announced. On this occasion the subject proved to be a great draw. The University students, scenting an attack on the Word of God, a delightful prospect to the heart of the unregenerate in every place, assembled in great numbers. A learned doctor of philosophy had come to tear the Bible to shreds; they must be present to testify their approval right boisterously.

When Dr. Baedeker appeared on the platform he was welcomed with a storm of applause. When he invited his audience to bow their heads for a few moments' prayer, they stared at each other in astonishment. The early portion of the address was listened to in significant silence. It took the young fellows some time to realise the exact situation. Then they became restless, noisy, insulting, and the assembly broke up in a violent storm. A huge mob waited in the street for his emergence from the hall.

"We will fling him into the lake when he comes out!" they cried excitedly. Passing out through the rear of the premises, he escaped their fury and reached home in safety.

The next Saturday he again applied for the use of the hall for the following day. It was refused.

"We dare not let it to you for such a purpose if you offered twice the rent," said the proprietor.

Nor could he hire any other hall in the city. Had he been an infidel lecturer instead of an evangelist it would have been an easy matter to have secured a platform. Dr. Baedeker, however, was not to be beaten. He sought out the Methodist Chapel authorities. They had already heard all about him, and readily allowed him to conduct his meeting there.

The doctor laboured in Zurich on that visit for nearly twelve months, holding services in a theatre for the most part. God never allowed his enemies to do him the slightest injury, or to daunt his adventurous spirit. He has preached in Zurich many times since then; and the fruits of his work are yet to be seen upon the shores of the lake in which the opponents of the gospel would gladly have seen him drown.

The following letter furnishes a-delightfully, significant sequel to the incident just narrated:

"ZÜRICH V, *2nd December,* 1896.

"MY DEAR FRIEND,—No sooner do I place my foot on foreign soil than my time seems to be filled up with happy testimony to the Lord.

"Arriving in Paris, my time was already laid out, and filled up with happy service.... On Saturday morning I arrived in Bâle, and gave my dear friends the opportunity of serving me with, oh, so much love! Meetings had been arranged in various places; and I found myself taken care of, and just conducted about, so that I felt like a blind man or a little child, without a care!

"Here I have my meetings in the same large hall which they once refused to let me have the second time. Now they give it me free of charge! Last night I had my first meeting, which was well attended. This afternoon will be a Bible-reading, and every day the same till Sunday. To-day my subject is 'Faith and Life.' I send you the advertisement that you may pray for these great opportunities.

On Saturday I hope to go to Glarus, in the most grand mountain scenery; but I have scarcely time to look at the mountains!..."

The protecting care of God was similarly manifested in the city of Dresden. Every night the doctor held gospel meetings in a hall in the city, the congregations being drawn in part from the roughest class. A Baptist minister, fully in sympathy, came and lent his aid.

"I want your especial help to-morrow night," said the doctor to him at the close of one of the services.

"I will do my best to serve you. What is it?" said the pastor.

"Will you take the service here?"

"Shall you be absent?"

"I have been asked by some friends to conduct a meeting on an island in the river Elbe to-morrow evening; and as I never neglect to enter an open door, I should like to go, if you will take my place here."

"That will I, with pleasure."

"Here, then, is the money to pay the rent of the hall. The landlord lives next door."

Dr. Baedeker departed for his island meeting, and the Baptist pastor took his place as arranged. It was the custom to pay the rent for the hall each night after the meeting, when desired so to do. At the close of the service the pastor proceeded to the house adjoining for that purpose; and after doing so, turned to re-enter the hall on his way home.

"You need not go back there," said the kindly landlord. "There is a way out here. By this side street you will reach your house more quickly."

The pastor thanked the landlord and departed.

On the following morning Dr. Baedeker received a visit from the police.

"You had a narrow escape last night, sir," said the officer.

"Please explain!" said the doctor.

"A band of evil-disposed roughs had planned to maltreat you as you left the hall at the close of your meeting," said he. "They were very astonished that you did not appear. Where did you vanish to?"

"I was not even present at the meeting," the doctor replied.

"But a meeting was held, and they were in waiting outside."

"The Baptist pastor took my place."

"If they had caught him it would have been the same. How did he disappear?"

"How God delivered him I cannot tell you, for I was not there," said the doctor reverently.

"We must see that you are protected," said the officer as he departed.

How God delivered the pastor also, Dr, Baedeker afterwards learned from the lips of the pastor himself as narrated above; and the two servants of God united in giving praise for His providential care.

The doctor used to tell a story of, an adventure that befell him on one of his visits to Transcaucasia. He had gone to conduct a series of meetings in a remote Armenian village among the mountains. It was in the end of December. The lateness of the season, the awful loneliness of the district, the risks of sudden snow-storms blinding the venturesome travellers, and covering tracks and way marks, all united to make the enterprise unattractive to those who knew the country. But the villagers had pressed him to visit them on so many previous occasions, when it was impossible for him to do so, that he could no longer resist their importunities.

On a memorable Christmas morning he bade them farewell, and with his Armenian interpreter and guide began, the return journey. A few of the Christian brethren of the village accompanied them a little way to point out the track. Presently these also were left behind, and the two proceeded on their way alone.

> **SCRIPTURE TESTIMONY**
>
> *God answers prayer*
>
> LUKE 18:7 · JOHN 15:7 ·
> ACTS 12:5 · JAMES 5:15

How long they had been wandering in the wide solitudes before the guide became apprehensive that he had lost his bearings, I cannot remember hearing. The signs of night oncoming were beginning to appear—and when night falls, it falls suddenly in those regions—when the Armenian at length stood still and said:

"I can go no farther. I am spent. We have lost our way: and we are walking in vain!"

"Is there nothing you can recognise? Nothing to show us our whereabouts, or the direction we should take?" the doctor inquired.

"I have been seeking and watching for some sign or mark in Vain! Alas! We shall perish here of cold before the morning comes. The sun will set in a few minutes."

"Then let us just kneel down where we are and tell our Heavenly Father about it."

"Alas! that I was so foolish as to venture on such a journey, so unfamiliar, and at such a season!"

"God can take care of us and direct us. We will pray about it."

"Most likely we are many hours' journey from a human habitation, and my limbs are very weary. I shall never see my home again!"

"If you don't know the way, God does. Come, cease lamenting, and we will pray together.'"

The two men knelt silently side by side for a few minutes, Then the doctor turned his face to heaven, and prayed in his glad familiar manner to Him in Whom he trusted with such triumphant faith.

"Father, we cannot be lost, for we are in Thy hand all the time, and under the shadow of Thy wing. Thou knowest the way that we take. Send us help in our need, and guide us to safety!"

The prayer was interrupted by the distant barking of a dog.

"Listen! There is our Father's answer," said the doctor. "Praise His name, He hears, and does not keep us in suspense."

The welcome sound inspired the fainting guide with new strength. They turned in the direction of the sound, and following it, arrived as the night was closing in upon them, at a small Tartar encampment.

The surprise of the Tartars on seeing the new arrivals was very great.

"How did you come this way?" they inquired. "We never see travellers hereabouts in December. Are you not afraid of the snows?"

"My Master, who guided me here, can control the snows so that they shall not hurt us; and you can see He has done so, for no snow has fallen."

"Who is your Master, then?"

"Herr Jesus!"

And there and then he opened his mouth and began and preached unto them Jesus. Although they were Mohammedans they listened attentively to their venerable visitor, who afterwards told how they gave him and his guide the best entertainment in their power. His Christmas dinner that evening consisted of a piece of the common hard black bread, eaten by the Tartars, and a pomegranate! Writing home to his wife on the following day he told her he imagined the feastings in England; and was certain that nobody at home ate their Christmas dinner with more gratitude and joy in the Lord, than he ate his. In the morning, with much good will, the Tartars sent one of their number along with them to put them into the right road.

This story of the doctor reminds me of another and a similar circumstance, which he sometimes narrated to illustrate how God delivers, when He is called upon in the day of trouble.

In Odessa, on one occasion, Dr. Baedeker was preaching in a public hall. His subject was "Prayer."

"God hears us when we cry to Him. You may be quite sure of it. He has promised to answer prayer, and He will never break His word."

Immediately upon the close of the address, a man in the hall stepped forward and asked permission to speak.

"Sir," said he, "what you have told us to-night about God answering prayer, is perfectly true. I had a godly mother; she had an unworthy and wicked son. One day I was riding on horseback across the steppe, far from home, when my horse put his foot in a hole in the black earth, stumbled, threw me over his head, and broke my leg. When I regained my senses, to my horror I beheld

SCRIPTURE TESTIMONY

God answers prayer

LUKE 18:7 · JOHN 15:7 ·
ACTS 12:5 · JAMES 5:15

my horse trotting away in the distance. Here was I left all alone on that vast steppe, no house nor human being within sight as far as eye could discover. Death threatened me, and I shuddered—wolves, probably or else starvation. In my agony of body and of mind I thought of my mother's God, and closed my eyes to pray.

"'O God, if there be a God,' I sobbed out, 'have mercy upon me now! I am doomed to a dreadful death if Thou wilt not have pity on me. Send me help, save me, I entreat of Thee, O my God!'

"A flow of hot tears kept my eyes sealed. My brain was reeling; I was on the point of fainting with terror.

"'Little father, what is the matter with you?'

"A real human voice was sounding in my ears; but at first I thought it must be the voice of God. I opened my wet eyes in wonder. Before me stood two peasants. They bent over me pityingly.

"'We must help the poor fellow,' one said to the other.

'See, his leg is injured—broken!'

"'How came you here?' I inquired, with astonishment

"'We were resting by the road-track yonder, and seeing you fall, hastened to your help.'

"'It was God who sent you to me,' I said.

"'We do not doubt it. You have need of us,' the peasants replied, reverently baring their heads and making the sign of the cross, according to their custom.

"With the utmost care, for every movement gave me agony, the two men conveyed me to their dwelling on the steppe. There for weeks I was nursed, until my fractured limb was healed and strong again. After such an experience as that, he would be a rash man who would undertake to convince me that God does not answer prayer."

How God delivered Patwakan Tarajantz, an Armenian Christian, in the massacre at Baku, four or five years ago, was a story that Dr. Baedeker delighted to tell. Tarajantz was one of the doctor's most useful travelling companions and interpreters. He accompanied the doctor on his second journey across Asia; and proved himself

Patwakan Tarajantz and Family

invaluable, not only in his ready and effective translation of the addresses, but also by his careful, intelligent, and untiring attention to the doctor's personal comfort and well-being. When the outbreak of violence against the Armenians in Baku arose, Tarajantz was at his home in that town, with his wife and family of ten children. From an upper window of his dwelling he looked down upon the turbulent mob of Turks and Kurds, and heard their fanatical threatenings as they hurried hither

> SCRIPTURE TESTIMONY
>
> *Deliverance from enemies and circumstances*
>
> LUKE 1:71
>
> *God sends an angel to help, deliver, or comfort*
>
> LUKE 22:43 · ACTS 12:6-11

and thither in their work of incendiarism and butchery. The sky was ruddy with the glare of burning buildings; the air filled with cries of hatred and screams of agony and terror. The savages were slowly but surely approaching his abode. They were taking the dwellings house by house. The residents in that quarter of the town were nearly all Armenians. Paying no heed to piteous appeals for mercy, they set fire to each house, consigning the occupants to a horrible death. It was only a question of a few minutes, and the turn of himself and his family would come. The poor fellow spent those few minutes in earnest prayer to God. Meanwhile the mob drew nearer. The anxiety was fearful. Now they are at his door!

"Down with the Armenians! Death to the Armenians! Burn them alive!"

Suddenly the bowlings and shoutings in the street below ceased. A stalwart Russian has taken up his position in front of Tarajantz's door.

"This neighbour is not to be interfered with. He is a good fellow. He is different from all the others. Pass along!"

The human tide of fierce fanaticism obeyed the authoritative word. It "passed along"; and continued its diabolical work at the houses that lay beyond. Of all the houses of the Armenians in that district, one only was not a charred ruin entombing the remains of the hopeless inhabitants—the dwelling of Patwakan Tarajantz. In the year before his decease, Dr. Baedeker intro-duced Mr. Tarajantz to the Brit-ish and Foreign Bible Society; and his name appears in the Report of that Society for 1906

> **SCRIPTURE TESTIMONY**
>
> *Do good to those who hate you*
>
> MATTHEW 5:44 · LUKE 6:27

as having received aid in the shape of a grant of copies of the Scriptures for circulation in Baku. To those who would eagerly have been his murderers, he is supplying the bread of everlasting life.

On one occasion, when on a visit to the Caucasus, Dr. Baedeker was the guest of a well-to-do Molokan who was the owner of a woodyard.

"It will be advisable for you to keep away from the woodyard," said his host. "I keep a savage dog there. The fact is, there are so many thieves hereabouts that I was obliged to put the dog there to prevent the yard being emptied. If my men are about, the animal is all right; but in their absence it is not safe to go near."

One day the doctor forgot the warning, and was halfway across the woodyard when he heard an angry roar, and turn-ing his head saw the huge brute making for him most savagely. Dr. Baedeker turned to run; but

> **SCRIPTURE TESTIMONY**
>
> *As we serve Him, the Lord will be our defense*
>
> LUKE 10:19 · 2 THESSALONIANS 3:1-3

stumbling, fell heavily upon his face, injuring his leg. The dog came rushing up, growling angrily, and sniffed him all over from head to foot. The doctor's heart went to Heaven in a prayer for protection. The growls became fainter, and ceased. The doctor lifted his head after a few minutes to see what his enemy was doing. There was no enemy there. The dog had trotted quietly back to his kennel. The doctor rose to his feet with difficulty, for he had sprained his muscles, and hobbled back to the house, the animal being an interested, but by no means hostile, spectator of his movements.

The astonishment of his host and the family that he had escaped so easily, was very great, for the brute showed no mercy to strangers; but the doctor thought of Daniel, and said to himself:

"The jaws of dogs are as easily shut as those of lions. Praise be to God!"

"God holds the winds in His fists, and the sea-waves in the hollow of His hand." This was a very prominent article of his creed. He had certainly plenty of opportunities of putting it to the test, and was amply satisfied as to its soundness. One instance in his experience, recorded in his letters, was his first voyage between Saghalien island and Japan. On landing at Hakodate he heard of an English doctor who was in hospital there. He also had come from Saghalien a few days earlier; but had been shipwrecked On the way, and in the rescue had had two of his ribs broken. While Dr. Baedeker was detained at Hakodate for a boat to take him on to Yokohama, a violent storm arose on the east coast of Japan. News arrived of terrible disasters to shipping; one boat, a sister-vessel to that which had carried him to the island, was wrecked, and all on board were lost with the exception of one man. Also a Turkish man-of-war, cruising in the same waters, had foundered in the same storm. It was with feelings of deepest thankfulness that the veteran, on sailing out of Hakodate harbour for Yokohama, observed that God had made the storm a calm, and that the Pacific had heard the Divine "Peace be still!"

When Dr. Baedeker counted his blessings, he always put the protecting care of his Heavenly Father high up upon the list.

CHAPTER VIII

Hostile Priests and Active Police

THE shrewdness and tact of Dr. Baedeker helped him many a time when he found himself in a tight corner. In many places, in the early days, the police

paid him most careful attention, and he puzzled them. He was quite accustomed to the sight of the police-spies lounging around the door of his hotel. There was no lack of police spies in Russia. They followed him along the public thoroughfares, and waited upon him among the domestics of the households in which he was a guest; reporting fortnightly to their superiors all they had heard and seen. What an atmosphere of suspicion and deceit in which to live! Dr. Baedeker was often greatly amused by their transparent tricks and antics.

On one occasion, at Riga, when he was as yet unknown, he had engaged a hall, and issued his bills for public services. In due course he was visited by the officers of the law.

57

"You must not hold services here," they explained. "Do you not know that religious services other than those of the authorised churches are strictly forbidden?"

The doctor was perplexed. He reflected a moment or two.

"Might I deliver a lecture instead?" he inquired.

"We do not see any objection to that," the official replied. "Lectures are not prohibited by the laws."

"Then I will lecture!" said the doctor.

"Quite right!" said the police; "but there must be neither singing nor prayer." The old bills were covered by new, announcing that on a certain evening Dr. F. W. Baedeker, of England, would lecture on "Sin and Salvation!" The night proved to be extremely unfavourable. Sleet and snow, and the inky darkness, suggested that but few would brave the discomfort of the weather to attend. To his amazement when he arrived in the vicinity of the hall, the street was blocked with vehicles of all descriptions. The people had come in crowds from far and wide. The aristocrats of the district were there in force, as well as humbler folk. Barons and counts, with their ladies and families and attendants, jostled with trades folk and toilers, all eager to hear the wonderful words of life, to us so familiar, to them so strange and so Divine. Meetings were held night after night in that district. The lecture on "Sin and Salvation" was repeated again and again. In one public hall two thousand, and in another, three thousand persons thronged to hear the Word. A friend of the preacher translated the addresses into Lettish as he proceeded, and many others beside the police said "Quite right!"

The bitterest opposition encountered by the doctor was that of the Lutheran clergy. In many places these men manifested a distressing alacrity to set the machinery of the law in motion to obstruct his work. It might be imagined that he was a dangerous sower of sedition and revolution, or a pernicious corrupter of the morals of the people, instead of a messenger of the Divine pity for sinful, sorrowing humanity; so zealously did they breathe out threatenings and slaughter against him. Nor were they content with the sober if severe methods of prohibition, arrest, and imprisonment. Again and again they made shameful appeal to the passions of the mob, and by discordant bands, bell-ringing, and even attempts at personal violence, endeavoured to frustrate his efforts to save and bless among the people. The Lord mercifully protected him from harm, and marvellously opened up opportunities for his ministry in most unlikely quarters: but the story of the opposition and persecution he endured is disgraceful reading to fair-minded men. We will allow the doctor to tell his own story.

"The Lutheran pastors at Wasa showed great sympathy. They seem to be of a different make from the Baltic pastors. It is clear that it is not the Lutheran Church as a whole that is against the free gospel."

With this generous recognition of brotherly interest as an introduction, we will proceed to the narrative of one of his visits to the Baltic provinces.

"*Stockholm, May 27.*—I have not wanted happy openings for service. The journeys by rail and sea give me the needed intervals of rest. When in St. Petersburg, Count S. gave me letters of introduction to the Governor at Riga, to the police-master at Mitau, etc. Yet I dare not be confident. My only confidence must be in the Lord. He has helped hitherto.

"Everyone tells me that the doors in Reval are shut. But I am not inclined to take it for granted. The poor people need the gospel; and they do not get it, either in the Lutheran or in the Greek Church. The trouble will be to find it in one's heart to leave, the places. I know you pray for me, my darling wife, and many others also; and this is a great comfort to me. Although hitherto the Lord has put open doors before me, I can only rejoice with fear, and I need His guidance from day to day. Yesterday the Lord gave His messages with much power, and laid hold on some souls."

"Hark, near Rival, June 14.—I arrived here all right. Had a good sleep on the way. A carriage, with four abreast, met me at the station."

"June 20.—I intended to leave Reval to-morrow, the doors being closed against me. But to my great surprise and joy, a door was opened by the Esthonian brethren for me to speak again in their large hall (Bet-Haus). A second meeting was announced for yesterday afternoon, but the pastor went to forbid my doing so again. The poor Esthonians were in great sorrow, and a neighbour opened a large garden for meetings to be held in the open air. We had two meetings yesterday; and for to-day two meetings are announced in the same place, at five and at eight p.m.

> SCRIPTURE TESTIMONY
>
> *Religious zealots opposed to the Gospel*
>
> ACTS 13:45 · ACTS 14:2

"The Lutheran pastors have not yet learnt that the gospel has to be given to the people by anyone whom God sends. 'Let him that heareth say, Come!' In their view there is no room for any labourer who is not ordained by their own Lutheran priests. The dear Esthonians beg and entreat me to remain longer; but I dread creating an opposition party. I may return this way again. In Helsingfors, two professors of the University translated for me. Here in Reval they do not want me. Only the poor hear gladly. It keeps one humble. Through evil report and through good report preach the Word!

"There was a large meeting this afternoon. There will probably be a larger one this evening. God gave the word, and there was blessing. Many decided for the Lord. Praise be to His name! I hope to start at five to-morrow morning for Kerro. God bless you, my darling!"

"June 21 (postcard).—I have had a narrow escape. The police were set upon us through the Lutheran priests when there were about 300 people in a garden to hear the gospel. The Governor quashed the accusation. The dear brethren here have to fight a battle for a free gospel. The Esthonians know what they want, and I trust they will get it in spite of all opposition."

"St: Petersburg, June 25.—I spent a full day at Kerro, and arrived here safely this morning... After the meeting was dispersed by the police, I had to appear at the police-office; but the Governor had given orders not to take any proceedings, and I was free to leave the place. I still hope to return to Reval. It is touching to see the dear Esthonians how they cling to one.

"I went to see the Governor. He was very friendly, and several times expressed his pleasure at having made my acquaintance. I told him he cannot stop me preaching the gospel. I must preach as long as I have breath; and everyone has a right to hear it. The Gospel of Christ is as free as the air we breathe. He fully agreed with me, but begged me not to do anything just now."

Here is a more cheering and creditable report from Livonia.

"Riga, July 11.—I had a full day yesterday. The Lettish people flocked together. I had three meetings for them with interpretation, and a German meeting besides. Speaking with interpretation gives one rest, and I did not feel over-fatigued.

"To-morrow I hope to see the Governor and find out what amount of liberty there is to be obtained. There is a new head of police, who might refuse me, but I have a letter from Count S. to the Governor, and I shall see what it will effect.

"The police are very vigilant. They even followed me into a private house yesterday where we had the German meeting, and asked the sight of my passport. It is really ludicrous."

"July 12.—I have just seen the Governor. He was friendly, and gave me a letter to the curator about my addresses, so that there is no doubt I shall have permission. He gave me also permission to visit the prisons, and introduced me to the head of the police for that purpose. Praise God for the open door! I shall go to the prisons to-morrow! Princess M. is coming to luncheon at one p.m."

The following is an idyllic picture:

"Reval, Esthonia.—-Although the pastors here shut the doors against me, the Master has effectually opened others, straight to the dear people's hearts. They flock together at a few hours' notice, by telling each other, and so the meetings are packed. The Esthonians have very tender hearts, and a little love shown to them even melts them to tears. You may imagine how the wondrous story of the cross moves them!

"In a country place, by the seaside, we had quite a concourse of Esthonian peasants, some of whom had walked great distances. The meetings were held under the great pine trees, squirrels walking quietly overhead while we were praising the Lord. It seemed a beginning of millennial peace and happiness. Many souls did, I believe, touch the hem of His garment, and the Divine power, undiminished, went out to heal as many as touched Him. We are having a happy time Of reaping here, the Lord be praised!"

The same spirit of intolerant interference with any effort for the amelioration of the moral and spiritual condition of the people was met with in Southern Russia. Here is an adventure for Christ in the Crimea, a district he often visited in his evangelistic tours:

"Sevastopol.—The cry I had sent up to the Lord for the thousands of workmen in this place has not been in vain. My steamer

will leave to-morrow for Odessa. I had hoped to leave to-day, but the Lord had work for me here. A boxful of New Testaments and Russ tracts has just arrived for me. They have come in the nick of time. Unpacking and circulating them was just a joy and pleasure. The hungry people went on their way rejoicing over their new possession. It is an awful weight of responsibility to leave soldiers, sailors, thousands of workmen in the dockyards here, without even the possibility of hearing the gospel. They are given up to their own devices; and as they have no one to show them any good, one cannot wonder that infidelity and nihilism result. How can it be otherwise?

"The place is full of flags. It is one of the crown holidays. I am very thankful for the splendid opportunity of giving Testaments and Russ tracts—no interference from anyone. How good it is of the Lord to guide one in a way that we know not! Oh, may the Lord bless abundantly the seed that has this day been sown broadcast! A dear Englishman who is engaged in the dockyards is a great help in distributing the Scriptures among the men. There is a very eager demand for the New Testament by the Russians. The four hundred which I sent him will not by any means satisfy the demand.

"The police-sergeant has just paid me a visit; and requests me to call at the police-station to-morrow morning-at nine, about the books I have been giving away. I will not post this till I know what the result will be.

"Praise the Lord, all is well! The consul has seen the vice-governor, and the affair is ended. The books have been distributed in great numbers—seed sown for eternity! The devil has been defeated. He is not allowed to pluck up the seed ere it can take root and grow up. Surely God doeth all things well! I have received my passport again, and therefore can now leave by the afternoon boat for Odessa!"

If the doctor had not been a foreign gentleman, able to produce letters of reference from the very highest circles in St. Petersburg, he would probably have been summarily sent to Siberia to end his days there. Russia, in enslaving the consciences of her subjects and darkening their minds by hindering the knowledge of God's Word, was unwittingly preparing for days of fire and blood. May God avert the calamity!

CHAPTER IX

In St. Petersburg Drawing-Rooms

HAVE you heard of the Russian *Velvet Book*—the *Barhatnaïa Knegat?* It is an important volume, preserved at the heraldic Office of the senate at St. Petersburg, and guarded with the most jealous care. It is the ancient genealogical register of the Russian nobility; and is called the *Velvet Book* from the fact that it is sumptuously bound in rich crimson velvet. Oh, what efforts have been made in past generations, by powerful and wealthy families, to get their names inserted in the Velvet Book! It was the highest pinnacle of the ambition of the Russian aristocrat. All the resources of influence and intrigue at Court have been employed to this end, and usually employed in vain.

But there is an even more select and noble register than the *Velvet Book;* and during the past thirty years many names inscribed in the earthly, have also been written in the heavenly roll, the *Lamb's Book of Life.* When Lord Radstock introduced his friend, Dr. Baedeker, to some of the noblest family circles in St. Petersburg, the doctor found among them warm-hearted, Spirit-taught, and consecrated souls not a few. These gave the doctor the heartiest of welcomes; so far as they were able, aided his evangelistic enterprises; and in some cases paid the penalty of their loyalty to their Lord by incurring the displeasure of the Emperor and enduring exile from their native land.

The enemies of evangelical truth did not hesitate to point even to certain well-known princesses —widowed ladies—whose only offence was that of Daniel, "concerning the law of their God," and demanded their banishment. Their over-zeal in this instance, however, met with a stern rebuke from the Czar.

"Let my widows alone!" he exclaimed. And thenceforward they entertained their Christian guests, and held Bible-readings and prayer-meetings in their drawing-rooms, none daring to make them afraid.

It was in the palace of one of these noble ladies, Her Highness Princess Lieven, that Dr. and Mrs. Baedeker usually made their home on their many visits to St. Petersburg.

"Your room is all ready for you," wrote the Princess to him, in inviting him to visit the city.

From that city he writes home:

"I have arrived safely. The dear Princess fetched me, in her carriage, and gave me a hearty welcome. I was delightfully tired with travelling all night; but I had some business to transact in the city, and at six p.m. I dined with Princess M., who is always very affectionate. At 8:30 we had a Bible-reading at Princess G.'s, and it was past midnight when I got to bed. I am all right, thank God, this morning. Praise be to His name!"

On the following-day he wrote:

"If you had seen the hearty welcome I received at the station, you would have wished to share it with me. But you have a full share in the love of our friends here. The Princess, and Mr. S., Countess K.'s brother, met me at the station; and on my arrival at the house, Princess G. and the five children all greeted me most heartily.

"It is quite wonderful how the Lord continues His work here; and how the Christians love one another! I also get a very large

Her Highness Princess Lieven and Family
Rear: Prince Paul, Prince Anatol
Front: Princess Mary, Princess Alicia, Princess Sophie

share of their affection. All here are well and bright. Wilhelm, the head servant, has left, and a Russian, who last year was dismissed from his situation on account of his religion, has taken his place. The weather here is beautiful, with brilliant clear sky at night, and sunny days. Last night the lights on the banks of the Neva were beautiful to look at. The Emperor is now at Gatschino."

The room usually set apart for the use of Dr. Baedeker in the house of Princess Lieven was that known as the Malachite Hall, because of the magnificent malachite mantelpiece and pillars and cornices with which the apartment is decorated. This was the "prophet's chamber," and many honoured servants of the Lord have enjoyed the hospitality provided by the noble hostess in that beautiful room, among others Mr. and Mrs. George Müller. In the spacious white drawing-room the meetings were usually held, and times of refreshing from the presence of the Lord we may be sure they were. The doctor visited the malachite quarries or mines from whence the marble, ornamentation of this hall was brought, on one of his Siberian journeys. They are near Ekaterinburg, on the eastern slope of the Ural Mountains. The workmen were busy cutting and polishing some costly vases for the Emperor when he saw them. The hard green stone, most delicately veined, is exceedingly beautiful when polished.

By the kindness of the princess, the readers of this biography enjoy the privilege of a glimpse of herself and her family. Grouped around Her Highness are her sons, Prince. Anatol (in uniform) and Prince Paul, and her daughters Princesses Mary, Alicia, and Sophie. Princess Mary devoted herself most heroically to hospital-nursing among the wounded in Manchuria during the recent lamentable war. The hearts of the Christian people of this country will sympathise deeply with Princess Lieven and the family in the terrible sorrow that has befallen them in the death of Princess Mary, as the result of a sad accident at Lausanne in January last. From her dying bed the dear girl stretched out her arms, and said joyfully, Jesus calls me! These were her last words ere she passed into His presence. May the God of all comfort sustain the beloved friends in their bereavement.

Count Bobrinsky has already been mentioned. His conversion to God was the result of a casual conversation with Lord Radstock. He held an important command in the Crimean War, where he was prostrated by typhus fever. His illness made him reflective, a seeker for truth and for God. For twenty years he prayed to "the unknown God;" then came the glorious enlightenment of his soul, and then followed twenty years of delightful consecration and service, until his home-call came. He threw his house open for the study of the Word of God and for prayer. Every Saturday evening at eight o'clock two meetings were held simultaneously, one for young people and another for those of maturer years; the evening's exercises finishing with the drinking of tea together, after the Russian manner, at eleven o'clock. It was usually in the small hours of the morning when the gathering broke up. The doctor and his wife described the proceedings vividly. What most impressed us about the meetings, was that when the address was concluded there was a startling scratching sound heard from all parts of the room—and a smell of sulphur! What could it be? It was only the ladies striking matches wherewith to light their cigarettes, preparatory to a conversational discussion of the address they had just been listening to. It was the custom. Count Bobrinsky felt, however, that the themes and interests that brought them together were of too sacred a character to be contaminated by tobacco smoke. He therefore begged that his fair guests would impose upon themselves a self-denying ordinance in the matter, His view was ultimately adopted by all save one dear Countess, who plaintively protested that she was too old to sacrifice her little indulgence. She was permitted, therefore, to scratch and to puff to her heart's content.

A notable drawing-room meeting conversion was that of Colonel P. His wife was first brought to the Lord, and, like the rest, threw her drawing-room open for gospel meetings. Her husband disappeared from St. Petersburg to avoid the gatherings of Christians, hiding himself for about two months on one of his provincial estates. At the end of that time he said to himself, "I will return to the city. The meetings are surely over by this time. I shall be quite safe." As he stood on the steps of his mansion in St. Petersburg, to his surprise strangers and acquaintances greeted him. They also were going in. What was the matter? To his annoyance he learned that a meeting was about to be held in his drawing-room! There was no help for it. He must join them, and show hospitality to his visitors. At the close of the meeting the gallant Colonel was on his knees. "It was as if a ray from heaven," he afterwards declared, "shot through my breast. I arose from my knees, ran into my bedroom, and gave myself to God."

The doors of the country houses of the Russian nobility were open to Dr. Baedeker in all directions. He was, by no means keen about accepting invitations, unless there was opportunity for work for his Divine Master. Here is his feeling about it:

"I have had a few days with Baron S. and his wife. He is a friend of Princess X., and he urged me to stay with them. Visiting idle country people does not do me any good. I would much rather live on dry bread, and have my hands busy in the Lord's work, than feast on luxuries and be idle. Here the doors are effectually shut for me. But the Lord has begun to work amongst the people, and I am very thankful to pray for them."

The same resolute "one thing I do," is seen in his observations in respect of a wedding-feast to which he was invited, and where he would have been an honoured guest. To his wife he writes:

"I have this morning written to the Baron and to his sisters. Your letter confirms me in my judgment. I told them that I should be glad to be present at the wedding if it could be on the 12th or 13th; but I must beg to be excused if it were put off to the end of the month. I do not like to let time pass away which may be of vital importance to some poor prisoners. I ought to be in Russia by the 5th."

This is a delightful variation of the parable of the marriage-feast and the excuses of the invited guests. Even the claims of high-born bride and noble bridegroom must yield place to the sighing of the prisoner and the imperious call of duty.

In addition to the drawing-room meetings, and arising out of them, the method of personal interviews with inquirers and others was most fruitful of blessing. Extracts from one or two letters will suffice to give an idea of the opportunities that God gave to him of exercising his ministry in quarters not usually accessible to the evangelist.

"*St. Petersburg.*—This is the Emperor's birthday, and this is my last day here. I propose leaving for Berlin to-morrow. My proposed visit to the Grand Duchess did not take place. She was obliged to be with the Empress. But I went yesterday at her wish, and had a long talk with her, in which she seemed much interested. Poor unhappy woman, she poured out her griefs to me! I was able to speak very freely to her, and to pray with her, at her request. The interview lasted more than an hour.

"I also had a good time with the —— Ambassador and his wife. They were both much interested; and General W., who was present, equally so. My time has been well filled up, and now I have a German meeting at H., and one later in the white drawing-room in this house. The children are all well, but the Princess herself is ailing. The Countess S. begs to be very specially remembered to you, and many others also. Young Prince L. has been a great help to me in translating. He is a naval officer, and has come out quite on the Lord's side.

"I have been interrupted by a call of the —— Ambassador. He seems concerned about his own soul, and about the religious training of his children.

"There were good meetings yesterday. Several were helped and blessed. The Grand Duchess sent a pressing message begging me to give her an hour to-day, from four to five. So I have decided to stop another day. One or two other people beg to see me also. This is a fruitful field for quiet continuous labour; so many inquiring souls, and no one to show them the way plainly.

"My visit to Count X. was not satisfactory. He always professes to be a believer, but one feels that there is no real foundation, and no real turning away from sin. The Countess gave me an introduction to Countess W., whom I called upon, and had a long and interesting conversation with. Her husband is a man of great influence at Court, and she is a large-hearted, true Christian who does much good.

"The dear friends here are most loving and kind. To my great surprise Princess X. also arrived here from her island home. She is suffering from some internal complaint and has sent for the priest Joharin from Cronstadt to pray over her. You know she never left the Greek Church. However, she is a very kind loving sister in the Lord, as you know. The Count and Countess B. are here. I called on them, and the Count called on me this morning. I am trying to write, but letter-writing here is beset with many difficulties. Just now the third visitor has left me, and I am to have the Countess F. at 3 p.m. All make many inquiries after you. Princess G. has you very much in her thoughts.

"Yesterday a brother came to our prayer-meeting who had been in prison for eight months. He said the Lord had blessed him more than he could tell during his imprisonment. Next Sunday I am asked to preach in the American chapel. I had a good full day yesterday, both afternoon and evening. The Lord's work is deepening and spreading. Praised be His Holy Name!"

Part of his harvest safely garnered, awaited the doctor's joyous arrival in the Holy City of which the Lamb is the light. Here is an instance:

"Dear Baron H. has lost the youngest of his two remaining sons. One died last winter, and now his brother has passed away. He was a bright and happy Christian. When I was there, he and his brother had many questions to ask me, and I was much struck with the definiteness of purpose the younger one showed. His heart was set on being the Lord's servant, and he drank in every word of God with eagerness. Now he is in the presence-chamber of the King, and his questions will all be fully answered. Baron H. writes as only a man of God can write. He and his dear wife are looking up and beyond life's parting scenes."

The following is a characteristically Russian experience:

"Here I am stopping with Countess B. It is a fine country house. Her son, Count S., came to meet me, and persuaded me to visit them here. On our way from the station the sleigh overturned in a snow-drift. I was thrown out in the snow with the Count and all the luggage on top of me. But we were unhurt, and they soon put it all right again.

"Yesterday we called on Countess K., a Christian lady who lives eight verst from this, with her two young daughters. We drove in sleighs; Countess B. and I, in a sleigh drawn by four fine horses, and behind us Count S. and his wife in a sleigh drawn by two. As the country, roads and all, was covered with snow, Countess K. sent two men on horseback in front of us to point out the road. So it was quite a cavalcade.

"At the prison it was touching to see the attention and eagerness of the men. They were so thankful for the New Testaments, only there were none for the Tartars. I also had two meetings with

Russians in the town. The room was crowded, and the Lord gave entrance with power to His Word."

Also this, from St. Petersburg:

"At Reval I had permission to hold two public addresses in the Exchange Hall, which on each occasion was crowded with a most eager audience. You cannot think what a joy it is to be permitted to feed hungry souls.

"On Friday I went on a visit to my dear friend the Baroness Uexküll. Some neighbours were invited to meet me; also the Esthonian peasants came on two evenings to listen to the gospel by interpretation. We had happy fellowship in the Word. Yesterday we drove over the deep snow in a sleigh, the bells chiming joyfully, to visit one of my spiritual children who is very dear to me, but who had backslidden. The Good Shepherd has sought and found His straying child; and it was a great joy to me to see her return. I dined with her and her husband, and saw her three children, who stroked my face.

"Now I am safe here in my very comfortable quarters at Princess Lieven's. My days will be well filled up."

A proof of the affectionate solicitude with which his St. Petersburg friends regarded the doctor is found in the incident of the fur coat. Worn and enfeebled by frequently recurring attacks of fever, and depressed by low vitality and the harrowing scenes he had witnessed in his prison visitation in the Caucasus, he arrived in St. Petersburg at his home in the palace of the Princess Lieven. He writes:

"It is a great relief to see some bright faces again, and to see the Lord's work prospering. I am enjoying the rest, and am fast gaining strength, and throwing off the effects of the fevers. You know how well I am cared for here, The kind Princess proposed

Dr. Baedeker in Russian Attire

that you should come and stay here, and that I should make this
my centre of operations.

"This evening the Princess very confidentially said she wanted
to give me a new fur coat. I told her I had no need of one."

But Princesses, when they have really made up their noble minds,
are not so easily put off. There was some discussion as to what might
be done to the one the doctor was wearing—a beautiful sealskin, the
gift of Colonel Paschkoff—in order to make it still more comfortable
and serviceable against the severities of the Russian winters; but the
Princess quietly determined, like the-Master Himself, "to provide some
better thing." What happened to the original overcoat after it was
"packed up, to be taken home" we have no record; but in a few days
a magnificent new one, of black bear fur, with a cap of Kamtschatka
beaver fur, found its way into his possession. The doctor's comment is:

"Is not all this wonderfully good of the Lord? May He bless
her more and more!"

You may see how the doctor looked in his new bear fur coat and
beaver fur cap in the picture.

I am tempted to add another delightful little incident, for the sake
of the young people who have to endure the ordeal of the examina-
tion-room. God give you, dear young friend, such success as He gave
to young Prince Paul.

"The two sons of the Princess have gone for a tour with their
tutor. They are good boys, an honour to their name, and will
soon be young men. The second, Prince Paul, gave a capital
testimony before the tutors and professors. When the result of
the examination was known, and they told him he had passed,
and passed well, and praised him, he said before them all, 'No
praise is due to me. I prayed to the Lord; He has done it all!' He

went to the examination with the utmost calmness, assuring his mother that she need have no anxiety. He felt sure the Lord would bring to his memory the facts he needed in order to answer the questions. And God was gracious to him."

CHAPTER X

Descending into Hell

THE awful conditions of Russian, and particularly Siberian, prison life have been sufficiently described in detail by other writers, particularly Russian and American. It is not my object to harrow the soul and to bemire the imagination of my readers by quoting their words. The coarse animalism from which the common decencies of civilisation are absent, the overpowering stenches, the swarming vermin, the incessant noise and unrest day and night, the unfeeling guards, the fearful overcrowding, the sickness, the chains— all combine to make a hell upon earth, in which many thousands of our fellow-creatures have been condemned to spend their lives. What it must have been to men—and, oh, to women!—of refined tastes and delicate sensibilities, who can tell! When you add to the physical torments, the utter absence of all moral restraints, the working of lawless and ungovernable passions in vile speech and revolting conduct, the impossibility of escape even for a moment from the "human demons," to use Dr. Baedeker's own words, that are your appointed companions by day and by night, you will admit that imagination is utterly baffled to conceive the infernoes that some of these places used to be. Dr. Baedeker gratefully reported that the Russian Government was making great improvements; "but," said he, "Russia is enormous; larger than the whole of Africa; larger than the United States and Canada; and the evils of centuries are not rectified in a year."

Look down into the crater of this lurid volcano of human misery, agony, and despair. The unhappy sufferers are criminals, of course. But the offences against the laws of their country and of God are of the past; their mute quivering anguish is of the present, a long-drawn-out horror. The man who takes a few drops of human sympathy and Divine compassion to cool these torments, is a veritable angel of God. When the doctor first went over the Urals in 1889, and saw Siberia, he sent home his impressions in a letter written on board the S.S. *Fortuna* on the mighty Obi River between Tomsk and Tobolsk. His travelling companion and interpreter on this journey was Count Scherbini. He writes:

"We are again on the water *en route* for Tobolsk, which we may reach in about a week. The prisons at Tomsk are simply horrible beyond description or imagination. The number of prisoners has been increasing for some time. Every week a transport arrives from Europe with 600 or 800, and about 300 or 400 are sent eastward. There are three prisons, one where work is done, containing about 300 men; the second, where the prisoners are confined for a lengthy period, containing 1600 or 1700; and then the worst of all, containing 3400, who are kept in sixteen wooden sheds, each crammed with about 200 or more. As the weather is fine they walk about in the yard, and there is always a crowd of all nationalities: Russ, Jews, Germans, Esthonians, Letts, Finns, Grusinians, Tartars, Khirgese, Persians, etc., women and children as well. It is a sight to make one's heart bleed, to see little children fondly embracing their father who is heavily chained; and mothers who have three or four children with them, all looking sickly from exposure and privation. The atmosphere with such a number of people is simply poison; but they told me it is not so bad in summer, when they can spend their time in the open air, some even sleeping out on the ground. But when rain and cold weather begin, and they are confined to their sheds, then they sicken and die off in great numbers.

"But the horror of horrors is the sick-house, which we visited yesterday. The doctor has had typhus fever sixteen times in thirteen years. There were about two hundred and fifty sick. A large contingent of them are Caucasians, who do not readily acclimatize themselves, and who die very fast when winter sets in. There were in the wards all kinds of illnesses placed together: typhus, smallpox, diarrhea, consumption, besides lighter complaints and chronic evils: some lying on mattresses on the floor, some in the act of breathing their last, whilst we passed through the wards. The atmosphere is pestilential, even though there was access of fresh air through windows and doors. Many patients were laid in the open yard on the grass.

"We saw a band of three hundred marching off eastward. The officials suggested that we should follow them to the first etape, about thirty-five verst distant. This we did the next day, starting about 9 a.m. We arrived at the etape about 2 p.m. We saw these three hundred men after their first day's march, and it was a pitiable sight to see the many sick and footsore—the legs, and feet swollen and festering with walking in chains. They took me for a medical man, and showed me all their sores. I had several opportunities to preach to them very freely; both in the large prison, in some of the sheds, and in the yards where they flocked together. They listened most attentively, some in tears, to the word spoken. Never have I seen such congregations anywhere, and such eager attention and gratitude.

"We returned from our expedition to the first etape, and went the second time to the large prison, and to the sick-house. Whilst we were there, a woman had run away; and many of the officers and guards were out in search of her. So we had quite full liberty, no one interfering, to speak to the prisoners, both publicly in the yard and more privately and individually through the open window in the office, while they crowded around outside and asked questions.

"The officials are all very kind and helpful. They are at their wits' end to know what to do. The Governor, whom we visited yesterday, had sent a telegram to St. Petersburg to say the prisons were overcrowded, and to stop any further arrivals. But St. Petersburg is 'far away,' as the saying goes; and it is plain enough that the pulse of Siberia is not felt in St. Petersburg, although the Government is supposed to govern all Russia, both in Asia and in Europe. All our New Testaments and portions have been disposed of, except some Tartar and Persian copies. Tomsk is the worst prison I have seen; and unless prompt measures are taken, the numbers may easily reach 7000 or 8000. Great numbers run away. It is calculated that about 50,000 escaped prisoners are in Siberia. A few of these find work and bread; but the great mass go about begging and robbing, or they starve. It is simply a slow death they are condemned to.

"Even the free colonists fare very little better. They are sent to settle in impossible places; and the fearful passport system needlessly aggravates their condition. There seems to be no way out for these poor people. Oh that God would move the Emperor's heart to give liberty to these oppressed ones!

"A poor old man, a Pole, came into the office whilst we were there, to hand in a petition. The clerk snubbed him very rudely, and I remonstrated with him, upon which he softened down, and spoke kindly to the old man and explained the rules to him. We gave the old man a little money to buy tea. You can form no idea of the utter misery on every side. They might easily rise up in a body and take their liberty; but this would simply mean starvation; whereas now they get food.

"The Lord has been marvellously gracious to us. I am well in health, and so also is Scherbini. We went into the prisons and into the sick-houses, trusting in His keeping. Psalm 91 was given me in power! Praise His Name!

"The steamer has just called at an Ostiak fishing station to take in a great quantity of dried and salted fish. We saw a little of Ostiak family life. A baby lay in a wooden box which was suspended from a beam. The mother and another woman were seated on the ground sewing. To the mother's great toe was tied a string, the other end of which was fastened to the cradle, and so she rocked the baby. They are much like Eskimos, not specially handsome in face or figure. I am sorry to say that they will do anything for drink, which is their curse.

"This journey by river-steamer is monotonous and wearisome, but I use every opportunity for conversation with the people on board."

Our pity for the prisoners and horror at their fate may possibly be qualified in most instances by the consideration that they are offenders against law, and have been justly sentenced. But what shall be said respecting the innocent men doomed to this worse than death? On board the steamer, on a return journey down the Obi, were a passenger and his wife, with whom the doctor had some conversation. They were very weather-beaten and prematurely furrowed and aged. They were exiles returning to Simpheropol in the Crimea. Dr. Baedeker found considerable difficulty in drawing them into conversation. Their long solitude and remoteness from civilised society had made them distressingly shy and timorous in the presence of human-kind. But the doctor was long familiar with the rare art of unlocking hearts and inspiring confidence; and presently the exile told his sorrowful story; He was an engineer, and was unfortunate enough to be acquainted with certain persons implicated in the conspiracy which resulted in the assassination of the Czar Alexander II. The assassins were condemned and executed. He was arrested on suspicion of complicity, but nothing was brought against him except the fact that some of the plotters were known to him, and that he possessed a printing-press. For these high crimes he was condemned. He was first kept in solitary confinement for sixteen months in a St. Petersburg prison, his jailers watching his every movement night and day. He was never permitted to utter a word. This awful ordeal ended, there began the march to Irkutsk in Siberia, by etape. He walked every step of the dreadful journey in chains, except the passage by barge on the Obi; and at its end passed into a prison-house, where he spent four years. His faithful wife bravely followed him, enduring cruel hardships on the way. At the end of four years he was liberated and permitted to reside in a hamlet near the prison, where for the further term, of six years he and his wife toiled for a scanty subsistence, pinching themselves in every possible way to save up enough money to pay their journey home at the end of their term, if their petition to do so should be granted. The Emperor was indulgent. Permission to return was given, and the two timid, bronzed, enfeebled exiles were on their way back to the dear spot where once their home stood and their friends lived— Simpheropol, where he will be under strict police supervision for the rest of his days. Of course their prospects in life were ruined, and they must begin life afresh; but their hearts were joyous in their newly-found freedom. "He looked a nice quiet man," the doctor said. The moral of the story appears to be—Avoid the acquaintanceship of everybody, who is likely to know anybody else, who is likely to speak to anybody else, on the subject of the murder of an Emperor, before it is accomplished!

It is the runaways who meet with the most terrible fate. It is utter madness to try to get away. Dr. Baedeker speaks of one case that he met with. The convict attempted to escape. The guards appeared so lax and the gate so temptingly open. But he had not reckoned on the vast distances, and the hopeless solitudes, and the pitiless frosts, and the cruel hunger. He was brought in with frozen limbs, which had to be amputated. By the aid of crutches he might have been able to

Fixing Fetters on Convicts

hobble if only he had possessed hands to hold the crutches. As it was, he had to be satisfied with painfully crawling on his mutilated stumps on the sloping bed-benches of a Siberian prison-kamera for the remainder of his days.

One bright gleam of light illuminated this valley of the shadow of death, to Dr. Baedeker; and that was the hearty good will and genuine sympathy with which the prison officers, from the Governor to the humblest warder, entered into his work. In some prisons the Governor stood by his side while he addressed the convicts, and at the close urged upon them the importance of earnest attention to what they had been listening to. In most cases this was superfluous; for the men were already overcome with emotion; but the interest shown in his efforts he gratefully appreciated.

Outside the prison-walls also, the doctor received much cheer of a similar kind.

"Your mission is certain to result in much blessing," said a General, a Military Judge, with whom he travelled on the steamer. "God give you good speed! You have my earnest prayers."

Even the cab-drivers and carters, who carried his great boxes of books rendered him help to the utmost of their power when they learned his errand.

"The Lord has borne us on eagles' wings; and His loving-kindness has followed us and gone before us all the way."

CHAPTER XI

Excellent Fishing in Dark Waters

AS has already been seen, Dr. Baedeker needed a mighty gospel. He required to preach an Arm that could reach the lowest, a Heart that could love the most unlovely, and a pardon that could rescue the most evil. Forty years' experience with His message, abundantly proved its sufficiency.

"I find excellent fishing in the dark waters of the prisons," he wrote home. "It is happy service to carry His messages from ward to ward, and pour it into ears that are eager to listen. I do not hide anything; but openly declare that the gospel of God's grace is for all men. No one dares to stop my mouth. With a few exceptions the officials have offered the greatest facilities, some of them helping me like brothers. The expression of loving sympathy breaks down many a hardened stouthearted criminal. One—convicted for the fifth time—fainted away when told of God's love to sinful men."

There was absolutely no chance for a convict in Russia. Every man and woman in the land must possess a passport, and produce it on demand. If convicted of any offence, the conviction was recorded, on the document. The passport might be renewed a dozen times; but the record of the offence, great or trivial it mattered not, was always transcribed upon the new passport. The poor fellow could never get away from his former evil deed. It dogged his footsteps with the grim tenacity of a sleuthhound, until he found the one hiding-place from its torturing persistency, the tomb.

"Once a criminal, always a criminal," was the merciless formula insisted upon by the horrible passport system of the Czar's dominions.

When in Siberia at the prison of Krasnojarsk, whither the doctor had gone on his usual errand, a young convict was told off to assist him by carrying his boxes, and opening and arranging the Bibles and portions which were to be presented to the prisoners. Dr. Baedeker entered into conversation with his helper, to whom he was attracted by his frank and amiable manner.

"I am grieved to see a young fellow like you, here. How did it happen?" he inquired sympathetically.

The young man's face became overclouded.

"It was just a moment of strong temptation. I yielded. I acknowledge I acted very wrongly, and am much ashamed of myself. May God forgive me!"

"What was your crime?"

"Incendiarism,"

"Your own dwelling?"

"Yes."

"For what cause? With what motive?"

"The old lure. The insurance money. It was the gold that tempted me. I thought I should not be discovered."

"But you were discovered!"

"Yes, and I am here."

"God witnessed your sin as well as human witnesses."

"I know it. I am truly penitent. I have acknowledged it. May He forgive me!"

"He is able to save, even to the uttermost. The blood of Jesus Christ His Son cleanseth from all sin. Let the wicked forsake his way, and return, and He will abundantly pardon."

"Thank God it is true. 'He will abundantly pardon.' I have nearly served my sentence!"

"That is good news."

"I will live a different life, God helping me, when I am released."

"Where is your home?"

"I have a brother in a high office under Government in the Baltic Provinces. You would not think it, but I am of noble birth!"

"Of noble birth?"

"Yes; of titled family. Am I not a disgrace to my connections? But I mean to retrieve my position and my good name. I will give them joy and pride in me yet, if I live!"

"You are young. You have your life before you, See that you use it well, and for God's glory."

"That, by His grace, I intend to do," said the young convict; and they parted.

Three years afterwards Dr. Baedeker visited the great prison at Irkutsk, near Lake Baikal, in Eastern Siberia. One of the first of the convicts who attracted his attention was the young fellow with whom he had had such bright conversation in the prison at Krasnojarsk. The cheerfulness had vanished from his face, and, instead, his features had set into a hard, almost fierce expression. He turned away as the doctor approached him.

"Oh, how sorry I am to see you here," said the kindly visitor.

"Please don't speak to me."

"But you must let me still be your friend. How came you here?"

"I have no friend in the world; nor in heaven either."

"Yes, you have a Friend in heaven, come what will."

"God knows I tried to do right when I was released. But I could get no help anywhere. Nobody would employ me. They asked to see my passport. That was enough. My relatives closed their doors against me. I could not even get food to satisfy my gnawing hunger. I should have died of starvation in the open streets if I had not got myself rearrested. So, you see, here I am; my body in prison, my soul in utter darkness and despair."

"The Lord Jesus cannot be kept out of prisons, praise His name!" said the doctor, with a glad smile. "He is the friend of sinners. This is just the place for Him, and you are just the very man for Him. Look up, dear lad! If man will not forgive and pity you, He does! And He has sent me here, after you, to tell you so! There is no record against you on your heavenly passport. The Blood, makes that whiter than snow! Your sins and your iniquities will I remember no more."

And thus tenderly and sweetly the veteran evangelist poured the oil and the wine of gospel consolation and hope into the cruel wounds in that poor young prisoner's heart. He had been a bright and hopeful specimen of Russia's young manhood, but the bruised reed was broken by the harsh passport law, and the merciless gates of his country's prison had closed on him for ever.

"Why do you come to us?" exclaimed some of the astonished prisoners of Saghalien to him, on the occasion of one of his visits to that island of dark despair. "There is no hope for us!"

We have nothing corresponding to Saghalien in the compass of our civilisation. For a generation the Russian authorities have sent away to that terrible island of fog and ice, the most desperate criminals of the Empire. Toiling in chains, and formerly branded with hot irons on the forehead and on each cheek, and surrounded for the greater part of the year by a frozen sea, escape was hopeless, and existence a living death.

"Why do you come to us? This is the place where there is no hope."

"If that is so," he answered, "forgive me for not coming to you first of .all. The place where there is no hope is just the place for the message of God's salvation."

Tears coursed down the cheeks of the faithful servant of God as he told of Him to whom of old the publicans and sinners drew near; who was able to save to the uttermost. And the sullen hardened cut-throats of the most remorseless penal settlement of Czardom, listened wistfully to the music of the gospel's joyful sound."

"If I had many lives," he said in an address at Weston-super-Mare, "I could not wish to spend one of them otherwise than as I have spent this one, in carrying the good tidings of great joy to those thousands upon thousands of hapless, hopeless men, who sit in darkness and the shadow of death all their days. You comfortable English people in your homes of love and luxury, secure in the enjoyment of your civil liberties, and favoured above all nations with gospel light and privilege, must not imagine you are the only men and women whom God loves. These gangs of Russian criminals have surely a share in the pity of the Heavenly Father's heart, and a place in the provisions of His infinite grace in Christ Jesus."

"What have you got in these cases?" inquired the surly captain of a Russian river-steamer in the early days of his itineracy.

"Bibles and Testaments," replied the doctor.

> **SCRIPTURE TESTIMONY**
>
> *True disciples give one hundred percent to the work of the Kingdom*
>
> MATTHEW 25:14-30

"Likely story that!" grunted the captain, whose suspicious mind probably imagined dynamite and infernal machines. "What are you going to do with them?"

"Distribute them in the prisons at —— and ——."

"Do you mean 'sell them'? Convicts have not much spare cash."

"I mean to give them freely. Convicts have souls."

"Oh, you give your goods for nothing, do you? Would you object to my examining a case or two?"

"You may open as many as you like," replied the doctor.

"Here—you!" calling a sailor who stood near by. "Break open one of these cases and let us see what is inside."

The case was opened. The captain reached down, and brought out a plainly bound copy of the Word of God. He dived deeper, tumbling out the contents to the very bottom. Bibles all—nothing besides!

"Open that one!" he shouted. The sailor obeyed; and the case was carefully examined throughout."

"Put the books back," he ordered, and turned and walked away. Presently he returned to the doctor.

"Who are you, sir?" he inquired. The doctor gave his name and his English address.

"Did you say from England?"

"Yes."

"And you've come to this country to give presents of Bibles to our Russian criminals?"

"Yes."

"You get a good salary for your work, no doubt?"

"I receive no salary whatever."

"Who pays your expenses?"

"I pay my expenses from my own purse."

"You what?"

"I pay all expenses from my own purse."

"Well, I call that noble! You are a man of a million! I wish I might let you travel on this steamer free of charge; but, at least, you shall not pay a single kopek for the carriage of your boxes!"

The magnificent self-denying labours of this pioneer have made it remarkably easy for his successors in service, particularly the Bible Society's agents. The authorities were taken by storm. Here was indeed a man of a million, a man well-deserving of all the encouragement and aid that it lay in their power to render. It was not long before he had not only free access to all prisons, but also many privileges in travel, particularly on the rivers; and these privileges his successors inherit. "There is not," said Mr. Davidson, the Siberian agent of the British and Foreign Bible Society in 1895, "a single steamboat plying on any of the rivers of Siberia that would refuse to carry our men and books free of charge. We also enjoy a free grant for carriage of Scriptures on the Ural Railway. Such generosity on the part of the railway and steamboat companies deserves cordial recognition."

Year by year these valuable privileges have been continued to the agents of the Bible Society in Siberia and in some other parts of Russia until the present time.

Mr. R. C. Morgan's description of the doctor's methods, of which, for two months in 1901, he was an eye-witness, is most interesting.

"Dr. Baedeker, with his interpreter and friend, was always received, not only with the respect due to the authority by which he came, but with courtesy and appreciation of the object of his coming.

"In most cases the first interviews with prisoners were in rooms where a dozen or twenty, more or less, of the less serious cases, were gathered together. They were briefly addressed as sinners every one, whom God loves, and for whom He gave His Son to die. One thing was very clear—that the speaker loved them, and this always gave him an attentive ear.

"The officials, from the chief officer to the warders, and the two prisoners who carried the great basket of books from place to place, entered with zest into the distribution; and if a man who could read, of whatever nationality, was overlooked, he was pointed out, and a copy given him.

"In the first room we entered, we met with a surprise. The priest called the singing master, and the prisoners' choir (an institution usual in Russian prisons) sang some sacred pieces in a way which charmed us.

"Then we passed from room to room, Dr. Baedeker speaking in German through his interpreter, Mr. Patwakan Tarajantz, who translated the message into Russian, or Armenian, or Tartar. It was always a distinct and pungent declaration of man's fallen and sinful condition; no difference: the love of God; His unspeakable gift of His beloved Son; the only way of salvation through the blood of His Cross; assurance of justification and eternal life to all who come, unto God by Him—an international Gospel, as the speaker termed it.

"In one prison the first room visited contained about twenty men, all wearing chains, which clanked with a pitiful monotony.

"Some of the men in irons had committed murder, others had escaped from Siberia. Both these classes were destined to be deported thither. One of the men in chains was a fine-looking

young fellow, a military officer, who had been tempted to embez-
zle £250, and was sentenced to two years and a half of hard labour.

"Several of these heavily-sentenced men were Asiatics, speaking
languages in which no address could be given, for lack of an interpreter; but the few of them, and of other Asiatics who could read,
were asked to let their comrades hear the good news from the best
of books—the most precious book in the world, God's Book."

At Kichiniev in Bessarabia, after spending the night in the train on
a journey from Odessa, Dr. Baedeker called on the Governor in the
morning. He and his interpreter enjoyed the privilege of resting their
limbs for two hours in the antechamber until the great man was at
leisure to attend to them. At last, armed with a warrant under the
Governor's seal, they started off in a droshky for the prison. It is a large
building, very solidly built, walls four or five feet in thickness, and four
massive round towers. In the prison are cells for solitary confinement,
and underground dungeons, bare and dark and fearsome, where the
occupant may enjoy his wakeful and shivering nights upon the stone
floor in company with the awful vermin that swarm out in the darkness
seeking what they may devour.

The officials offered every facility and lent ready aid; and Dr. Baedeker and his interpreter had a good time with the prisoners. There were
Russians, Jews, Moldavians, and Roumanians. The men were marched
up in rows, and the presentation of a New Testament to such as could
read was preceded by a brief and earnest address, in which "the plain
gospel" was put before them. The doctor asked nobody's permission.
He just went on, and the authorities silently acquiesced. Very thankfully the men received the precious gifts.

"We have a murderer in our charge at present," said one of the
warders.

"Have I seen him?" the doctor inquired.

"No; he is in solitary confinement."

"Take me to his cell, please!"

Preceded by warders, the doctor stumbled down the stone staircase into the dark basement regions; and in one of the dungeons the object of their search was discovered.

"I cannot read, thank you!" he pitifully explained when Dr. Baedeker offered him a copy of the Scriptures.

"Here, then, is the very thing for you. You will be able to read this; and it teaches the truth it is most important that you should know."

The doctor produced a little "Wordless Book," and handed it to the condemned man.

The convict opened it, and gazed with perplexity upon its three leaves; the first, black; the second, red; the third, white.

"What is the meaning of these? I cannot understand," he asked.

The doctor's eyes shone with Divine light as he gave the familiar explanation to that miserable felon in the cell of doom. "The black leaf represents black sin— yours and mine. Sin against God

> **SCRIPTURE TESTIMONY**
>
> *Gospel is the power of God for salvation*
>
> ROMANS 1:16

and against man. Sin in the heart, and sin in the life—black as night; black as death; black with coming judgment. The red page represents 'the precious blood of Christ,' by which alone black sin can be cleansed and put away. , 'He was wounded for our transgressions; with His stripes we are healed.' The white leaf represents the perfect salvation of the soul through our Lord Jesus Christ; His abundant pardon of every sin, to those who repent and accept Christ; the complete righteousness that comes to the sinner through faith."

From one page to the other of the "Wordless Book" the eyes of the convict thoughtfully wandered, and his fingers trembled violently as he held the dainty little gospel messenger in the dim light.

"You are able to read that little book, are you not?" the doctor asked tenderly.

"Yes, I can read it, thank God!" he replied; and as he looked into the doctor's face, big unfamiliar tear-drops fell upon his chained hands.

"And thank you, sir, a thousandfold, for bringing such a message to such an unworthy wretch as I am!"

Hidden in the dreadful depths of these abodes of crime and despair, Dr. Baedeker occasionally met with one or more of the Lord's servants, condemned and imprisoned, and "taking pleasure in distresses for Christ's sake." Oh, what cheer he brought to the hearts of such! A brief extract from his diary, as a sample of many similar cases, may be given. It refers to an incident in his second journey across the continent of Asia, at the prison of Kabarowka, on the Amoor River.

"September 10.—Arrived at Kabarowka at 2.30 p.m. Visited prison, and had a good time. Found a brother two years and a half here for Christ's sake. Gave him ten roubles and a book of songs."

"And a book of songs!" That is delightful. We instinctively recall Philippi and the midnight duet and the conversion of the guards. "A book of songs!"

> "In darkest shades if He appear
>   My dawning is begun;
> He is my soul's bright Morning Star,
>   And He my rising sun."

"A book of songs!" Sing away, dear fellow, with all your heart! Your heaven has begun even in the Kabarowka hell. The repulsive kamera where you are herded with Russia's criminal offscouring, is none other than the House of God and the gate of glory to you! Sing out from your book of songs! The doctor was discriminating in his gift, or rather you were Divinely prompted in your request to him. You will set other hearts singing before you have got through your book. And we who read about it shall catch the echo of your solos and your choruses in the Heavenly City shortly.

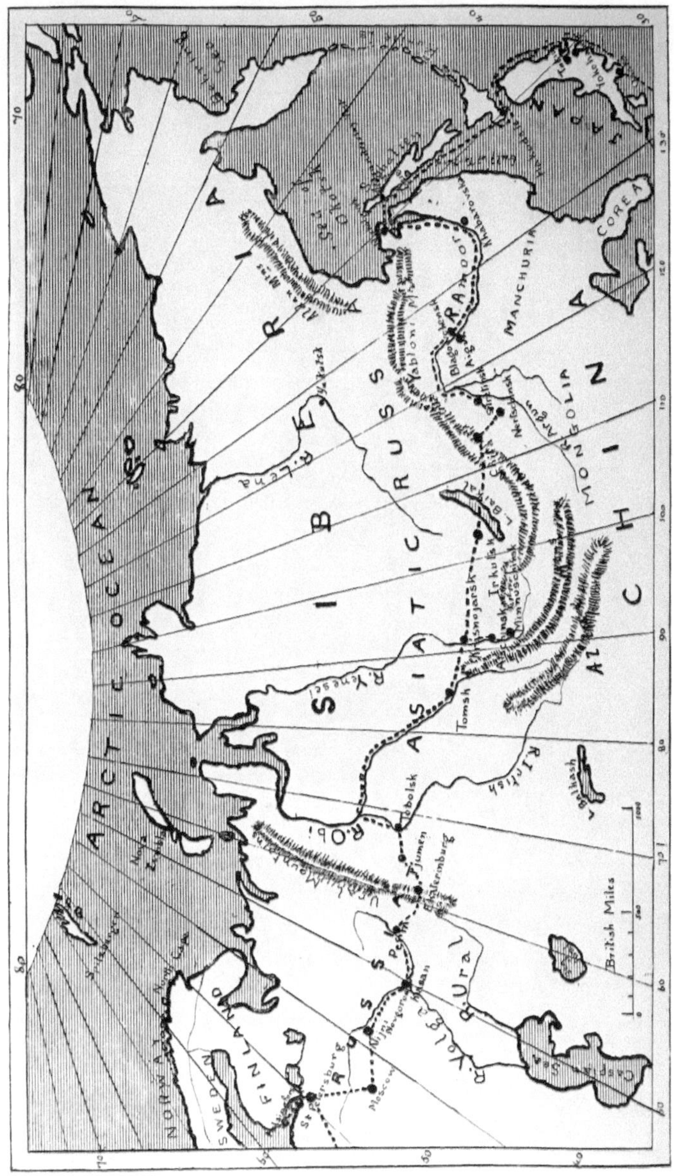

Dr. Baedeker's First Journey Across Asia

CHAPTER XII

Siberia from End to End

Dr. Baedeker's first journey across Asia;
compiled from his letters home

"WE have at last found a corner of the earth where the gospel has never in any shape been heard." Thus Dr. Baedeker wrote home to his wife from the Transbaikal prisons in the midsummer of 1890.

Since that year great changes have taken place in Siberia. There has been a considerable increase of the population owing to immigration. A railway track has been laid. The Government has expended large sums of money in opening up the Continent. And, above all, the terrible Russo-Japanese struggle has taken place. When Dr. Baedeker undertook his six months' zigzag outward journey across the two continents, the land eastward of the Obi River was practically uninhabited save by wild beasts in the enormous forests, with her and there a scant colony of miserable exiles, and in the awful heart of it a grim cluster of prisons, separated from each other by many miles of desolation, with a rough post-village somewhere in the neighbourhood of each.

Into and across these wilds this pioneer of the Cross eagerly ventured; impatiently traversing the vast solitudes to carry the bread of life to starving souls. In the following paragraphs we may accompany him, and look into the heart of the man also.

St. Petersburg to Perm

"Wierballen, Monday, April 28.—All has gone well. My luggage passed without difficulty; and I now send you my first lines from Russia. We have beautiful weather. Everything is bursting into green and blossom; but it is still winter, as you may see from the enclosed statistics of temperature which the Princess sent to me to Berlin.

"I had a very full day in Berlin, I was strengthened for it, and am feeling wonderfully well, thank our Heavenly Father. I feel so borne up by many prayers. Now I have another twenty-four hours' journey. The train is due at St. Petersburg at six p.m. tomorrow. It was remarkable how a nice corner seat was kept for me all the way. Although in a smoking carriage, it was pleasant and not overmuch smoke.... I know your prayers are paving the way for me, and giving me strength and all that is needed day by day. My love to all the dear friends who pray for me."

"St. Petersburg, Friday, May 2.—My time is always full when I am here; and I must use the early hours of the day to write. Yesterday I had a long talk with the Director's chief secretary, who gave me much information. He told me that the large prison in Irkutsk, holding 1400 prisoners, has been burnt down. Two prisoners were burnt to death. Three others are missing. To-day I am to visit some of the prisons here, and Mme. T. offered to be there on our arrival to translate for me. Yesterday afternoon we had a very good prayer-meeting, and last evening a Bible-reading

in the white drawing-room. We had a good and profitable time, praise God!

"Mr. C. is coming to take me to the prisons at 5 p.m. I have a children's meeting afterwards; and at 9 p.m. I depart for Helsingfors. I know you bear me up in your prayers."

"Helsingfors, Sunday, May 4.—Friends here are very warm in their love and sympathy. Last night we had a good meeting. Colonel S., who some years ago was converted at one of the meetings I held in this town, is also here on a visit, and his embrace was unusually sweet to me. I had never seen him since the time of his conversion. Just now we have had the breaking of bread in my room; and we were mindful of the whole company of the redeemed from all nations. My thoughts ran to you and to God's children at Weston-super-Mare.

"This afternoon and evening my time will be filled up, and to-morrow also. On Friday I went through one of the St. Petersburg prisons. Mme. T. interpreted. There were, of course, mostly fresh prisoners since my previous visit. No books could be seen of those which I had given. We had no difficulty in speaking to the men. There was a convict there who had committed fifteen murders. Apparently now he is under deep repentance.

"My permit for visiting the prisons has been renewed. I asked the Chief to word it so as to include an interpreter without giving the name of the interpreter. This gives me liberty to take whomsoever I may deem suitable, without any difficulty being raised as to his admission with me. The Chief was most friendly and kind to me, and readily acceded to my request. My name is thus a kind of latchkey for prison gates. I am very grateful for this; but I also know that the prayers of God's children are the power to which I owe so much.

"A large supply of books has been sent on ahead to Perm, Ekaterinburg, Tjumen, Tomsk, Irkutsk, and also to Nikolaiewsk, near

Saghalien, to await my arrival. May God give us much wisdom and power from on high, to meet all demands!"

"*St. Petersburg, Thursday, May 8.*—On my return from Finland I found your letters, and am thankful for their contents. I had a full time at Helsingfors. I meet the Russian Bible Committee this evening at 8. At 9 p.m. we shall have a farewell meeting in this house."

"*Moscow, Sunday, May 11.*—Arrived here at 10 a.m. yesterday. Mr. Kargel (interpreter, who it is arranged shall accompany me) had taken rooms for us both. We went at once to the large central prison, where the officials received me with open arms. The Governor of this prison always shows me much affection. We arrived in time to see a party of exiles, 400 men, women, and children, going off to Siberia, on the long and terrible march. We hope to go again to this prison to-morrow. There are about 3000 prisoners. Six times every month a party is sent off. A kind-hearted Moscow merchant gives to each exile on their departure one rouble—to man, woman, and child. There were some with three or four children. Some carried infants in arms. But not one was overlooked—for each child a rouble was given. An aged priest also gave ten kopeks to each. It was a sad sight to see them all. Knowing what I do of Siberia, I feel sure that many of these dear creatures, especially the children, will perish by the way. They can never reach their destination.

"Last night we had a delightful meeting in a private house. This morning we remembered the Lord's death, with nine or ten present. We have just said 'good-bye' to A——'s three boys. They are at school here. We took them with us to a dining-house. We have arranged for a gospel meeting at 5 p.m. The weather here is very beautiful."

"Monday, May 12.—This morning we went to the prison. The sight we saw was sad and sickening—about 800 men in chains. We were able to speak to them and present them with the books. We shall go again tomorrow to see a similar number; and then to the females' prison to see 300 women. The men we saw this morning are all going to Siberia. The prison here is clean and airy. There are no evil smells. I have sent forward seventeen boxes of Bibles by land, and four boxes by sea. May God bless each copy to the recipient! Mr. Kargel has been a great help to me this morning. He is bold, and speaks without hesitation. This is a great comfort to me. I trust the Lord will help and strengthen him."

"Nijni Novgorod, Wednesday, May 14.—We had a comfortable journey through the night. Leaving Moscow at 6 p.m., we arrived here about 9 a.m. On arriving, we drove with our box of books straight to the large prison, and without any delay we were allowed to visit and distribute to the prisoners about five hundred books. We then had dinner, and afterwards drove with our luggage to the steamboat quay. We have for the first time used the beautiful 'message' to make tea for ourselves. You would have liked to see us with it. It is quite a success, and will be useful for making tea, soup, etc, for ourselves on the way.

"I had great joy in finding that many people remembered us. A Tartar, who last year conveyed our boxes with books, came up to-day beaming with pleasure at seeing me again. Also the man at the steamboat office remembered me.

"At Moscow, and also here, some prisoners begged hard for money for tea. I was very glad to spend the gifts of Anne and Mary for this."

"Saturday, May 17.—There are on board our steamer about 500 emigrants—all very poor. They have left their homes in the province of Koursk, and are going to Tomsk with wives and little

ones. They have nothing to eat but bread. With this they drink hot water. They call it 'tea.' The children are beginning to sicken. They looked so starved, that I thought a meal of hot Russian meat-soup would revive them. The cook of the ship arranged to supply them, and they have all had a real feast.

> **SCRIPTURE TESTIMONY**
>
> *The righteous innately have God's heart toward those in need*
>
> MATTHEW 25:31-46

To me the feast was still greater, seeing them all enjoy it, and looking up to God, the Giver of all good gifts! The poor creatures are packed together in a dreadful manner. I am thankful that we are favoured with fine weather. If rain or snow were to set in, I do not know what would happen. God only knows what will become of them ultimately in Tomsk, in the frosts and snows. Many of the children will scarcely live to see their new abode.

"There are also some discharged soldiers who have served in Turkestan, and who are on their way home to Perm and Ekaterinburg. They are hardy fellows but as their food also consists solely of black bread and tea, they also partook of the feast. They are all very grateful, poor creatures! It cost me seventy-five roubles. We had many opportunities to speak to them about spiritual matters. Most likely we shall see their faces no more.

"The river Kama, a tributary of the Volga, is a fine broad stream, and pours an immense volume of water into the Volga. We shall be on the way until Monday. At Kasan we took a fresh supply of New Testaments, which we have given to the emigrants and soldiers who are able to read. The weather is magnificent. The country looks lovely, though here the trees are not yet in leaf. We are well provided with good food on board."

"*Perm, Monday, May 19.* — We arrived here this morning about eleven o'clock. We went at once to the Governor, and then to a large prison, in which are more than 600 prisoners crowded together in an unmerciful manner. We had them all together at first, and spoke to them about the purpose of our visit, and about their need, and the Lord's readiness to supply that need. When we began giving the New Testaments, it was impossible to keep order. We had to send them back to their kameras, and visit them there.

"I do not think I have seen a prison anywhere in which the men are crowded together as in this. There are two other prisons here, and we decided to visit at least one of them; if possible, both. There is only one train a day to Ekaterinburg. This evening a great number of the Russian peasants, our travelling companions, went off by train. But they will have to wait at Tjumen. I hear that some thousands of free emigrants are already at Tjumen waiting for the steamers to take them forward. And now 500 more have gone! Oh, what misery! It is past all conception. They are huddled together anyhow, with no control as to sanitary or moral measures. And the people themselves are so utterly ignorant. I don't know which is better, the lot of the prisoners or that of the free emigrants. A great many women have little children with them, even infants. It is really too bad of the authorities! If a few people were to gather together for a religious meeting, the police would at once interfere; but no notice is taken of any amount of immoral practices. The officials are most obliging to me."

Across the Ural Mountains. Perm to Tjumen

"Ekaterinburg, Saturday, May 24.—We arrived here safely by rail from Perm on the 21st (Wednesday), and had intended to leave for Tjumen on Friday; but it would be useless, as the river Obi is still icebound, and steamers cannot proceed. There is at

Tjumen a great accumulation of prisoners waiting to be taken on by steamer, besides the colonist-emigrants before mentioned. The latter are much worse off than the convicts. They have little or no shelter provided, and no food; and as measles have broken out among the children, people are not willing to receive them into their houses. I understand they are living in tents. Poor souls! This cold weather is enough to kill them.

"We visited the prison here, and found the prisoners were supplied with books from a stock which I had left with the Governor last year. The season is exceptionally late: we have snow-storms even now. There are a few English families here, whom I have visited. Mr. and Mrs. Davidson (of the British and Foreign Bible Society) are very kind. Mr. Davidson will travel with me between Tomsk and Irkutsk. It is a great privation to me not to have your letters. I hope to find a good budget when I arrive at Tomsk, God willing.

"This is quite a fine town. It is the centre of mining operations. Not far away are the famous Demidoff mines, where malachite is found, and from whence the malachite room in Princess Lieven's palace received its furniture. We went yesterday to see the stone-cutting works. Some very costly articles are being prepared for the Emperor. Some vases of a very hard stone are being cut. Some of the stones are exceedingly beautiful."

"*Tjumen, Tuesday, May 27.*—Arrived from Ekaterinburg this morning and were received with a most hearty welcome by Mr. Wardropper, whose guests we are. We have been very busy all day, and I am tired. Inquiring at the prison we found about 1930 prisoners. We then took the books and began the distribution. The men are terribly crowded together. Really, it is worse than I saw it here last year. I cannot think how they manage to live! There is, however, a great improvement in the sanitary arrangements. Tell this to Surgeon-Major Theobald when you meet him.

"We had great liberty in speaking to them. They listened most eagerly, and showed great gratitude. But we have only done a third part of the work here, and hope to resume it to-morrow morning. The New Testaments are received and read with intense eagerness.

"Nine or ten steamboats have been lying here in the river, frozen in. But the ice is now thawing. It is becoming quite warm and balmy. We hope soon to see green trees and flowery meadows. Hitherto there has been no sign of spring. The boats will be greatly crowded; so many passengers are waiting.

"Our train this morning brought a further 800 emigrants. You can form no conception of the scene. The rough sheds are occupied at night by the women and children; the men sleep as best they can on the ground outside. God have mercy on them! Misery such as I have never seen anywhere is crowded up and heaped together here.

"The prisoners are better provided for. Indeed, it often happens that colonists, at their wits' end, commit some crime in order to be taken to prison, where at least they get food to eat. A flight of pigeons are fed in the prison yard by the criminals, on the bread which they have to spare.

"I assure you it is a great trial to be without your letters for so long."

"*Tjumen, Friday, May 30.*—We hope to make a start at last to-morrow. There is an enormous accumulation of goods; so we are thankful to have our books forwarded thus far. We are better off than many others.

"This morning we went to see the poor colonists camping out in the open field; some of them almost starving. We had many opportunities of helping them with money, etc. It was a sorrowful sight to see them huddling together, lying on their clothes or on the bare ground. I am thankful to say the weather has turned fine and warm, so that they will not suffer so much. Nearly every day fresh numbers arrive by train.

"This afternoon we went on board the barge, where prisoners are placed in a kind of cage. They all knew us, having seen us in the prison. Whilst we were there the Russian priest held a service. All the prisoners listened and crossed themselves many times. It was the ordinary liturgical service in Slavonic, which very few understand. The responses are much the same as the Church of England service: *Lord, have mercy upon us.* The water was then 'sanctified' by a crucifix being passed through it, and the people, after kissing the crucifix, were sprinkled with the water."

"Our steamer leaves at twelve noon tomorrow I travelled in the same boat last year. The captain greeted me most warmly.

"The Wardroppers are very kind and hospitable. Mr. Wardropper kindly places a horse and conveyance at our disposal. This facilitates our going about. Their married daughter, who lives at Ekaterinburg, also showed us much kindness. Mr. George Kennan stayed here when he travelled through Siberia, and several other English speaking travellers. The condition of the prison here is far worse than even Mr. Kennan has described it. Still the prisoners are better off than the poor emigrants. Most of Kennan's papers have been cut out of the *Century* by the censor. The Russians cannot therefore learn the state of things in their own land.

"I begin to feel quite withered up from want of your letters. The time is so long. But I must be patient. I only hope you have not been anxious on my account.

"I can only cast all this upon the Lord, Who careth for us, and Who would have us to be without carefulness. It is not much more than a month since I left home, *yet it seems such a long time!* God guide our steps in His path, for His name sake!"

Tjumen and Tobolsk to Tomsk (about 1000 miles) by Steamer on the River Obi

"*Tobolsk, Monday, June 2.*—On arrival here we called on the Governor. He was very friendly, and gave us the names and situations of the several prisons in Tobolsk. We then visited them. Altogether there are about 1500 prisoners here, besides a great number of children, who with their mothers accompany the prisoners. Yesterday 480 were despatched by barge to Tomsk, and still there are so many. Great improvements have been made in one of the prisons where they give work to the men. But the numbers are overwhelming. Many of the men recognised me. They look upon me as their friend. Some had seen me in Tiflis in Transcaucasia. The officials also welcomed me gladly.

"To-day we had a thunderstorm, with heavy but warm rain. There are still heaps of snow lying about the streets, but spring is quickly advancing. To-morrow we hope to be busy in the prisons.

"As to-day is Whit-Monday and a holiday, in which nothing can be done, we hired a cab and paid a visit to the 'banished bell.' Because it had sounded for rebellious purposes, it had a 'sound' thrashing with the knout, had two of its 'ears' broken off, and was banished. It has never been restored to its place; but it is still used, and has an unusually clear sound at the slightest touch. 'Made perfect through suffering.'

"When we returned from our visit to the prisons, we found the Governor had called at our hotel and left his card.

"This place is full of descendants of Polish exiles, and many who have themselves been exiled from Poland. The winters are awfully quiet and dull, as the steamboats only run for a very few months. Part of the town is built on the hill, and the larger part on the flat along the river. There are many old churches, very ugly, but all looking clean in their whitewash. The streets are boarded with planks, as wood is abundant and cheap. Just now the boards are rotten in many places and need repairing."

"*Tuesday, June 3.*—We have had a very profitable visit to one of the prisons. The men listened eagerly to the gospel. We took longer time in each kamera, and the word was given and received in power. We hope to go again this afternoon and in the evening. The weather is beautiful. Everything is growing fast.

"*10 p.m.*—We have just returned after a very full and happy day. Several of the convicts asked for spectacles. We had the joy of supplying them, at fifty kopeks a pair (about one shilling). Several beg for money for tea; so one has many opportunities of showing kindness, and these little gifts are very gratefully received. This evening we had a large gathering in the prison-yard. The attention of the audience was most close and marked. Also the officials listen with the closest attention. I feel confidently assured of 'much fruit.'

"Many who had received Bibles or Testaments last year, came and showed them to us. Some had actually made cases of card-board for them, in order to protect them against wear and tear! God bless them!

"We have still work before us for two full days. The steamer for Tomsk is to pass by here on Saturday. I am weary with -waiting for letters. I have to exercise myself in patient waiting, and trust that all is well with you. It is good to be 'safe in the arms of Jesus!'"

"*On board Steamer on river Obi, Sunday, June 15.*— This is a long and tedious journey. We have now contrary winds. The river has overflowed its banks to such an extent that it looks more like a great lake than a river.

"We were kept at Tobolsk because the boat by which we intended to leave had no room for us. This boat took us as a special favour. The crowd of passengers is very great. We have

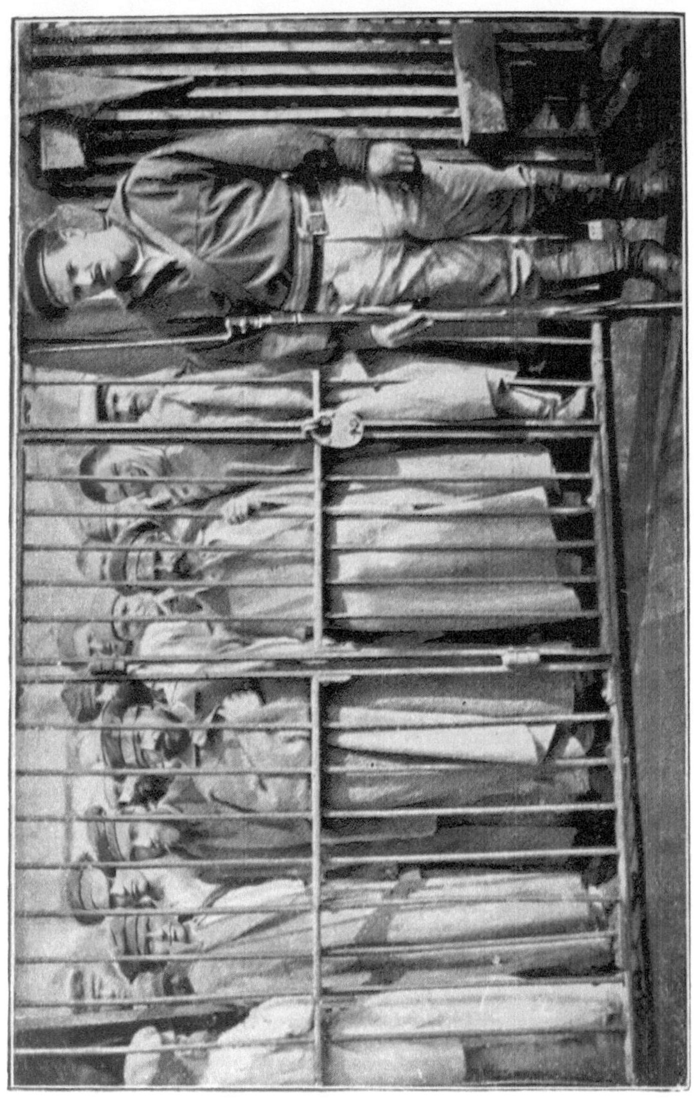

Convicts in Transportation

our beds in the common first-class cabin. Every berth is occupied. The ladies' saloon and the private cabins are all equally full. There is not a corner of privacy anywhere. The second class is equally crowded. Then there is a dense mass of deck passengers, the poor emigrants. These live chiefly on fish and dry bread, which they make into a soup. Their children look very sickly.

"The Governor came on board to see us off at Tobolsk. He introduced me to one of our fellow-passengers, a merchant from Tjumen.

"The directors of the Steamboat Company have again presented us with free tickets for ourselves and for the books we have with us. This is very kind."

"We have with us some wealthy Siberian merchants. One with wife and six children, two governesses, mother-in-law, and several servants. They have been in London and Paris, and are now going to spend the summer in their home at Krasnojarsk. Then there is a Russian Colonel and his wife, child, and nurse, who are going to Kabarbwka on the river Amoor. The wife looks delicate, and I fear is not used to roughing it, as she will have to. Then a scientific man from the Helsingfors University, with his young wife and his brother, who is a student. They are going for, archaeological researches to Kiachta, and farther into Mongolia. Some of the passengers belong to the mining districts of Transbaikalia—a gentleman, his wife, and two children, and some others with whom I can converse in German, and a little in English. Next to me in our cabin is Baron S., who is going to Irkutsk.

"The country on each side of the river is very uninteresting. The banks are overflowed. One sees great stretches of water, and tops of trees rising here and there out of the flood. Several of the Ostiak settlements have been abandoned. The inhabitants had to flee in their boats to higher land.

"When we stop here and there to take in wood for fuel, there is a great rush made by the passengers to buy fish, bread, milk, and ducks and geese. They are wonderfully cheap. In one place wild ducks were sold at three kopeks apiece, and wild geese at twelve or fifteen kopeks. Fish is less abundant at this time of the year; but they also are fabulously cheap. The wild ducks and geese are caught in nets, and killed by the hundred; the rivers are full of them. Also white swans are caught, and their skins preserved for furs!

"A poor exile came to us at one stopping-place. He had come from Riga, and had been sent to a miserable Siberian village, where he lived with a family of fishing people. At first, when we spoke to him in his own language, he could not answer us, having for so long heard and spoken nothing but Siberian-Russ. We had quite a long talk with him, and he seemed greatly affected, poor fellow! It is indeed hard to be exiled to such a place as this, a hamlet of perhaps a dozen wooden huts and a Russian church.

"Vegetation here is still far backward. I have this year passed out of Winter into Spring four times: the first Spring was in England; the second, at St. Petersburg; the third, on the Kama River; and now once more I behold the awakening of Nature; the willows are beginning to unfold their buds and show their leaves.

"The river is still rising, owing to the melting of the snows on the lofty Altai mountain chain to the south, between us and Thibet. There is no river in Europe to be compared with this, the Obi; or even with the Irtish, which is only one of its tributary streams. Although we have steamed up the river towards its source for a whole week, there is yet no perceptible diminution of the volume of its waters.

"In the mornings I am generally the first up. Then after reading and prayer each by himself, we have coffee, with bread and butter, and eggs. The butter has failed these last few days. About two p.m. we have our dinner, soup, two meats, and sweets. Then about seven p.m. we have tea, with bread and smoked fish. We still have tea and sugar in our "message;" and the smoked fish we bought at Tobolsk is very good. We retire early. The other passengers usually sit up late, to chat and smoke.

"I long to arrive at Tomsk to get into active service among the prisoners.

"This morning we had a breakdown of the engine. The anchor was cast in a wide wilderness of water while repairs were being effected. Happily after about five hours delay we are on our voyage once more. The first steamer, which left us behind as there was no room for us, has been stopped by ice. We have now overtaken her. All has been wonderfully ordered for us. We were able to make good use of our time in the prisons while waiting at Tobolsk, whereas if we had been taken on board, we should have had to spend the time in idleness."

"Monday, June 16.—We had again a breakdown, but the delay was not long. On one of the other boats a steampipe burst. The hot steam scalded great numbers of those on board; the third-class passengers were the chief sufferers. About sixty persons have died; so you may imagine the awful extent of the catastrophe. The Governor of Krasnojarsk with his family was on board, but none of them were injured.

"We are having great opportunities for conversation on religious subjects. A Christian farmer who is going to the Amoor River comes with many questions. Many passengers are attracted to listen to our answers. With several, an interest is clearly awakened. Praise God!

"We are dragging a heavily-laden barge behind us, and the current and the wind are against us, so our progress is slow. But I trust, that everything will be ordered according to His will, and for His glory.

"I can assure you it is a great trial to be deprived of your letters and to be so far away. I will send you a telegram on my arrival at Tomsk, and my great hope is that, I may find many letters, and good news. God grant that I may not be disappointed!"

"Tomsk, Wednesday, June 18.—We arrived all safe this morning. Mr. Davidson has met us. Your letters—! Praise the Lord for all His goodness! I am in excellent health, and trim for the journey that lies before us."

Telegram from Tomsk. *"Ebenezer!"*

"Tomsk, Friday, June 20.—The packages of books have not come to hand, and we must therefore remain here until next week.

"The prisons here are not overcrowded. In one, where last year I found 3400 men herded together, there are now 1000. In a second, where last year there were 1600, there are how 326. The third has its usual complement of 300. This is a great relief. I find in some places the men who received Testaments or Bibles last year. They greet me with a grateful smile, and show me their volumes, which they have read, and preserve lovingly. There are signs that the Word of God has hot been without effect on them. A spiritual spring-time is making its appearance.

"Yesterday morning we saw 250 men on the transport barge. We had a great opportunity to speak the gospel to them, and to give them books just before they started. The officer who was in command of the party was very kind, and we were greatly cheered.

"In the afternoon we went to the second prison, and had good opportunities there also.

"In the evening we visited the third prison. The convicts go out to work in the daytime: and only return about 7 or 8 p.m. We arrived at 8.30, and had a grand opportunity with them. There are a great many Jews among them. They are all most eager to receive the New Testament. None refuse it.

"We called yesterday on the Governor. He was very kind, and gave us for our journey a 'billet.' This will speed us on our way by securing for us a more ready supply of horses, and at a special rate. It sets forth that we are *under special command to visit the Siberian prisons and to supply the convicts with copies of the Holy Scriptures.*' If post-horses are not to be had, then the Government horses must be supplied. If these also fail, horses must be found anyhow, but somehow. So you see the Lord raises up friends and helpers in all directions. There is such a rush of travellers just now, so that this is a very valuable and important document. Also Kargel's passport had to be renewed. Through the Governor's kindness, this was done the same day; whilst ordinarily several days' delay might have occurred. Now we are only waiting for our books. Fortunately we have books enough for this place, and now we must go to visit the large prison. I will add a few lines when I return."

"*Saturday, June 21.*—Yesterday we had quite a field-day in the large prison. We did the work so far as we were able, very effectually going through the kameras one by one, speaking in each kamera, and giving a book to each prisoner who could read.

"Our books were not sufficient; nor was the time long enough. Mr. Davidson went with us, and was much touched by what he saw. We hope to go again this afternoon to do the remaining kameras, God willing.

"We had as much liberty as we wished for. After speaking at full length in each kamera, we spoke also in the open yard to the hundreds that crowded round. Ever so many petitions were thrust into my hands for a little help to the prisoners. Some were very pitiable cases. An apothecary, a well-educated man, had been robbed of his papers and of his clothes. He applied to the police for help. They gave him prison clothes, and the benefit of the prison for shelter!

"We found a young lad of sixteen in the prison in the company of all kinds of criminals. He looks clean and respectable; and I cannot bear the thought of leaving him there without making some effort to get him away. He has not apparently committed any crime. He got into bad company and lost his money in card-playing. He was discovered in the streets of this town practically destitute and without his passport, and was put into the prison, where he lives in the kamera with the others. I must speak to the Governor about him. Every day in the kamera will be for his ruin.

"We are anxious, Kargel and I, to go to Minuscinsk to visit a religious exile, a servant of my dear friend, Colonel Paschkoff, who was sent to Siberia, and who has suffered much for righteousness' sake and for the gospel.

"One gentleman from St. Petersburg is a prisoner on the march; and his wife, *a lady*, has followed him hitherto. Now her means are exhausted, and she is in utter poverty and despair. What -is she to do? A young gentleman (political convict) is on his way to Yakutsk also two ladies (political convicts) on the way to East Siberia. May God have mercy on them! Each one has his or her own history, as all sinners have. 'We have turned every one to his own way.'

"Now I must not write more. If we cannot speak or write *to* one another as often as we would wish, we will speak more often *of* each other to our Father in heaven.

"Davidson is a great help. So is Kargel. The Lord my Shepherd does not allow us to want. Praise His name!"

"Tomsk, Monday, June 23.—Still in Tomsk! But now our books have arrived at last, and we hope to receive them to-day. Then they will have to be packed for the long overland journey.

"I am glad Davidson is still here. He is a man full of energy, and a thorough business man. He gets on, too, with the authorities.

He will buy a waggon to convey the large packages of books. The waggon we shall have to sell on arriving at the other end. I had no conception of the difficulties and delays in the conveyance of luggage in Siberia. It will be much cheaper and quicker to buy a waggon and horses, and take the cases of books with us, selling the conveyance at the other end, than to have them sent by the public means of transit.

"Our time has not been wasted. Yesterday the German pastor asked me to speak in the church (Lutheran) after the morning service.

"At our hotel we had the Feast (Lord's Supper) spread for Kargel, Davidson, and myself. We felt cheered and strengthened by our communion. Our thoughts were with God's children in the homeland, and everywhere.

"While in the large prison, many convicts begged for a little tea. So when we called upon a tea merchant here we arranged for little parcels of brick-tea and sugar to be prepared, which we hope to take to the prisoners this morning. Also, we had to buy spectacles for some who cannot read without glasses. If we succeed in doing all that is needful to-day, we hope to start eastward tomorrow.

"Tomsk is a fine city and is fast rising to prominence in Siberia.

"On Saturday I called with Davidson on a Russian priest of high standing, a director of missions among the Mongols. He received us very kindly, and showed a warm interest in missionary work of all kinds. He invited me to become his guest; but this I was compelled to decline. The tea merchant mentioned above has an extensive business. He ordered from Mr. Davidson five thousand scriptures, which he will sell in his store.

"We have just returned from the prison, and have seen a party march off, with wives and children following, a most pitiable sight. We also visited the prison hospital. All is now very fair compared with last year. But the transports are now only beginning. They come in very fast, 700 or 800 every week, while twice a week parties of 300 or 400 leave for the far Eastern prisons and penal settlements. It is a sad sight to see these great numbers of men loitering about in the prison-yards.

"*3 p.m.*—I called again on the Governor to speak to him about the prisons, and to thank him for his kindness. He has released the lad, and given him into our charge. We shall take him with us to Irkutsk to his mother, who lives there. We now hope to leave Tomsk to-morrow. I shall try to write to you as often as possible, and to bear cheerfully the privation of your letters. I know you are praying for me."

Tomsk to Lake Baikal, by Road (about 1160 miles).

"We have purchased a tarantass for 130 roubles. Mr. Davidson has one of his own; and so we shall travel together.

"You can form little idea of what travelling by tarantass means. In appearance it is something like an old-fashioned family coach. The body of the conveyance is made of wicker-work lined with carpet. Overhead there is a moveable leather hood. There are no easy springs, alas! The body rests on poles——three or four long poles, the elasticity of which gives a slight relief from the jolting of the rough road, or rather track, which we follow as well as we are able. Three horses are harnessed abreast to each conveyance, and as the Siberian horses run very fast, the passenger must hold very tight until he becomes accustomed to the jerking and tossing. Where the roads are very rough, one is sometimes pitched about, up to the hood, or from one side to the other in a most unmerciful way. This conveyance is also our sleeping apartment, dining-room (in wet weather), and store-room.

"The hotel servants at Tomsk understand the packing of a tarantass. Their method is quite artistic; and their main object, to secure the comfort of the travellers in spite of the roughness of the road. About five hundred Bibles and Testaments, made up into parcels of forty books each, are first packed in the bottom of the conveyance as a sort of ballast. Then comes the remainder of the luggage—laid as level as possible. Then on the top is laid the mattress and pillows for the travellers to stretch on. One has to be provided with food, and tea and sugar; for at the post-stations only a samovar (a kind of urn in which water is heated by a central cylinder in which hot charcoal is placed) is to be had, and possibly eggs. You know how I like black bread. We can get it to perfection here. We also take a ham with us, some caviare, sardines, etc. Butter is not to be procured. Then the conveyance must carry boxes of grease for the wheels, and ropes and a hatchet, etc., to provide against breakdowns on the way.

"From Tomsk to Krasnojarsk direct is 550 verst; and from there to Irkutsk is 1000 verst, so you may picture to yourself what a journey lies in front of us. Still I do not for a moment regret having undertaken it; and I hope you are kept in joy and peace about my being so far away from you for a little while. From Tomsk to Krasnojarsk there are twenty-seven post-stations, at each of which we shall obtain a change of horses; and from Krasnojarsk to Irkutsk are forty post-stations.

"The work in the prisons increases in interest as we go on. The men and women are most grateful. We work systematically without any confusion or disorder. We have as much liberty as we desire—no one interfering, and both officials and prisoners listen most attentively. The real large prisons still lie far away beyond Lake Baikal.

"I cannot tell as yet how long my absence may be; but I hope that in October I may be allowed to return once more, and to see your dear face. I know you do not forget to pray for me, nor do

I forget you. God grant that we may ever be found of one heart seeking to glorify God, and to live to His praise. It is a sore trial to be cut off from all home-communication. I cannot say how we shall be able to get on beyond Nertschinsk, whether we may have to turn back, or go forward to the Pacific."

"Altschinsk, Saturday, June 28.—Through trials by land and by water, the Lord has helped us. We arrived here this afternoon, visited the prisons, and are now off again for Krasnojarsk. The roads in some parts are very bad. The crossing of rivers is very trying and difficult.

"In the prison here we found two men chained hand and foot, one a Lett, and the other an Esthonian. We had taken only Russian New Testaments with us. They entreated us pitifully for the book in their own language. We went back, and after search among the parcels found the books to satisfy their longings. May God bless them richly!"

Telegram from Krasnojarsk, June 30 "Ebenezer!"

"Krasnojarsk, Monday, June 30.—Kargel and I arrived here safe and sound after a journey by tarantass from Tuesday night till Monday morning, travelling with short intervals all the time. Our conveyance being full of books, and the roads for the most part being very heavy and bad, our progress was not rapid. But the three horses pulled us through the mud, over all the hills, through the rivers, etc. We have now about one-third of our tarantass journey behind us; but we have the advantage of the experience of the past week. We can get a good deal of rest by stopping at one of the post-stations during the heat of the day and travelling through the evening and night. The days are generally very hot,

and the nights very cold; but hitherto our gracious Father has sustained us in health and good spirits.

"In some parts the country is most beautiful; everywhere it is interesting. We have just emerged from dense forest, through which we have been travelling for two days; only the road cut through, giving us light, and a strip of the sky in front of us. Native grass is plentiful. Herds of cattle and horses abound. There is a most remarkable variety of flowers; the peony, ranunculus, and many others grow wild in superabundance. The turf is covered with them. There is a superabundance also of mosquitoes and small gnats. Just now the road here and there is being repaired; the many men at work scarcely know how to screen themselves from the little folk. They wear singular masks. We have to keep our tarantass closed to get free from their attacks.

"We visited the prisons of Marinsk and Altschinsk, and while here we shall visit that at Minuscinsk. There, are great numbers of exiles in this district. At one of the post-stations yesterday, a wreck of a nobleman came to ask for help. For some crime he had been banished to Siberia. He is now free from prison, and may live where he likes in Siberia. His sister is in prison in Irkutsk. He is on his way there; and when she is released they will live together and work for their maintenance. They are of a noble family from Lithuania. When I gave him some clothes and money, he burst into a flood of tears.

> ### SCRIPTURE TESTIMONY
>
> *Give to everyone who asks*
>
> MATTHEW 5:42 · LUKE 6:30 · ACTS 20:35 · 2 CORINTHIANS 8:1-2 · 1 JOHN 3:17
>
> *The righteous innately have God's heart toward those in need*
>
> MATTHEW 25:31-46

"The river Yenesei, beside which this town stands, is a magnificent stream, with mountains towering around us. The hand of man has not fallen upon the loveliness of nature here. The

A Siberian Tarantass

far-stretching forests filling the spacious valleys and covering the hillsides; the infinite profusion of wild flowers; the glorious summer sky, at times tinted and shaded with rainbow colours surpassing grand, are an unceasing charm to me. And then on the other hand prisons, criminals everywhere, thousands of them!

> "'Every prospect pleases,
> And only man is vile!'

"*Thursday, July 3.*—Davidson, who has been travelling with us, and who has taken charge of most of the books, fell behind because of the breakage of one of the wheels of the tarantass conveying the cases. A stronger conveyance had to be sought for, in the nearest village on the road. The weight even on this tarantass was plainly too heavy; we therefore bought a second, for twenty-five roubles, and divided the load. This also caused delay. There was no use Kargel's and my remaining, and as we were very desirous of getting to work in the prisons of Altschinsk, we pushed on ahead the same evening.

"On Sunday we rested during the day at a post-house. We had fellowship with all the church of God in the breaking of bread, and then went on during the night.

"On Monday we arrived here. We intended going to Minuscinsk by steamer up the river Yenesei, but Davidson had not made his appearance when the steamer started. I decided, therefore, on staying here for him, whilst Kargel went to Minuscinsk alone to see an exiled brother, and also to visit the prison there.

"Soon after he left, Davidson arrived. He had had another breakdown. Another new wheel was needed, and he was detained twelve hours in a village while it was supplied. We were most glad to see each other; but I am sorry I had to give up Minuscinsk.

"I am again alone. Davidson left last night, taking the books on the two conveyances, and the youth whom we took from the Tomsk prison. He had also brought with him a lady whom he found sitting by a river bank, waiting in the hope of being ferried across. For the greater part of the night she had been waiting there alone, pacing to and fro. It must have been terrible for her. She was following her husband—he is a prisoner—all the way from St. Petersburg. She has suffered much on the fearful journey. She is only twenty-seven years of age, but her hair has turned perfectly white. Her husband is here; and will be set at liberty to live in this district in a small hamlet about ten verst from this town. She is a real lady; but she is in very poor health, after her awful experiences. They do not know what to do. We have tried to encourage her. Certainly their lot is cast in a more pleasant place than if they had been banished farther on. Just now the country here is very pretty. In winter it is of course cold. It must be terribly hard to have one's home and associations suddenly torn up, by a rude and cruel force, and to be banished thousands of verst to a lonely land, to live in a wooden hut. We in England have no conception of this.

"In every place we pass through there are great numbers of exiles. For people of education and refinement this life must be dreadfully severe.

"I expect Kargel to return on Saturday. Then on Sunday we hope to visit the prisons here. We called there on Monday, and were told that Sunday would be the best day, as then the convicts would be at home. On Sunday night we hope to depart for Irkutsk, a seven days' rapid ride. Beyond Irkutsk we have still a long distance to travel. The chief prisons are beyond the Baikal lake.

"This is a journey which I shall certainly never make a second time. [*He did though!*] You will therefore sympathise with me in my desire to do what my hands find to do NOW, with all my might.

"We always take rest in the heat of the day, and travel from 4 p.m. till about 11 a.m.; it is much less fatiguing. We sleep, of course, in the tarantass. It is a novel experience. At first we found it most difficult to "drop off," for the rushing and the rocking and the jolting. But we are getting used to it now, and can sleep quickly and soundly.

"The fresh air is very exhilarating. The trees and the hills and the valleys are very fine, and the wild flowers charm us. But the mosquitoes are almost intolerable. Local people wear over their faces a kind of net made of horsehair, like a fine sieve. This, in the shape of a hood, is placed over head and shoulders, giving to the wearer a fearful appearance.

"Nature is here in her loveliest garb just now. I wonder how it is with you, and how the garden looks at home, the roses and the geraniums, the grapes and the figs? I wonder shall I get home in time to taste some of the fruits of our garden this year? I only wish I knew how you are, my darling wife, and what you are now doing!

"Let me show you the Krasnojarsk shops! Some of the merchants are enormously rich. Their houses are very large, with shops on the ground floor. These shops in some cases are almost like exhibitions. They sell all kinds of goods in the several departments, as at home, groceries, draperies, 'galanterie warren' (leather goods), ironmongery—five or six large shops under one roof and ownership. Provisions for the journey one must buy; for at the different post-stations nothing can be had except milk, eggs, and black bread. The samovar is brought in, and we make our own tea, and dish up whatever we have: sardines, cold tongue, and the like. We may sometimes get the people of the post-station to make soup for us. Vegetables are not to be had, except occasionally spring salad as a special treat. We do without butter, because we cannot get that luxury for love nor money. Travelling without delays, we may possibly do 200 verst a day."

"*Saturday, July 5.*—Kargel wires that he has missed the return steamer on the Yenesei from Minuscinsk, and must therefore return by land, a distance of 500 verst. So I must wait his coming.

"To-day I went to the prison and ascertained the number of the prisoners to be 486. To-morrow I hope to visit them, and present them with books. The chief assistant of the Governor understands French. I shall brush up my Russian, and my French sentences he has kindly promised to translate for me, so I hope to get on without my regular interpreter. I shall thus be ready to depart as soon as Kargel arrives. I long to push on. These days of delay are very trying. I began to think the enemy has his hand in it, to prevent our going into the darkest and most needy places.

"In this hotel I am well provided with good food. The luxury of washing is rather limited, while on the road. At every post-station there is in some hidden corner, a copper bowl holding about one quart of water. From this, the fluid trickles on one's hands on pressing up a wire which projects from the bottom. Underneath this is a brass basin to catch the dirty water as it drips from your hands. With this arrangement you have to do the best you can. In this hotel the servant offered to pour water over my hands, for my morning ablution. I made him understand that this did not satisfy me; and now I find in my room a basin and a jugful of water. They provide no linen. I also had to buy a feather cushion each for Kargel and myself, to use in the tarantass and on the beds. The bed provided consists only of a very hard mattress and a woollen plaid. With these you are expected to be happy.

"To-morrow morning I shall remember the Lord's death in the breaking of bread with the whole company of the redeemed. I know you will remember me, as I shall you."

"*Sunday, July 6.*—I have to-day been to the prison. The officer was standing ready to translate my French into Russian, when a convict called out:

"'Dr. Baedeker!'

"Everybody turned to look at the daring interrupter.

"'I know you, sir,' he Continued, speaking in German. 'I have heard you preach in prison several times. Please let me translate for you, and you can preach in German!'

"The prisoner was allowed to come and stand by my side. He interpreted very well, only he was rather timid in speaking to the other prisoners.

"In conversation with him afterwards, I ascertained that he was a Christian Jew who is at present in prison for being without his passport. He declares it was stolen from him. The authorities will send him by road and etape to his home province. He expressed great joy at meeting me again; and said that he was a believer who had sadly backslidden. I trust he will return to the Lord with all his heart, and be restored.

"There is in the prison a boy thirteen years old, the son of a murderer. His father attempted to escape- and killed two prison-warders, but he was shot, and died of his wound. The boy is getting into bad ways through the other prisoners. He is condemned to two years' imprisonment for concealing a murder at which he was present.

"There are several political prisoners here. One a clever man who can speak several languages. He is taken up with Tolstoy's teaching, but he accepted gratefully a New Testament. The prison is very clean, and by no means overcrowded. There is no interference with me whatever, on the part of the officials.

"It was no fault of Kargel's that he missed the steamer. The up-boat was twelve hours late in arriving at Minuscinsk. He had then to drive to a village some distance away to see the poor exiled brother. When he returned the down-boat had already left for Krasnojarsk. Now he has had a hard time of it, 500 verst in a postcarriage, which is extremely uncomfortable. I only hope he will not be completely broken down when he arrives here! We have had several heavy thunderstorms with downpouring rains. The roads must be bad. I fear he is having a trying time of it. I wish he were here; but I must commit him to the Father's care. He knows that we desire nothing better than to be His faithful stewards. His will be done.

"There are many Tartars here from the Caucasus, also Armenians, Jews, Germans, and one Esthonian, who with his wife expressed great joy when I gave them the New Testament in Esthonian. Of the Siberians, very few are able to read; of the women, scarcely any. What a blank their lives must be! They seem otherwise intelligent people."

"*Wednesday, July 9.*—Kargel arrived about two this morning after a very fatiguing journey. He has had some sleep, and we shall leave for Irkutsk this evening. It will be a journey of about seven days. The distance is 1008 verst, about 700 English miles.

"This morning we shall call on the Governor and speak a word for the Christian Jew, also for the thirteen-year old boy. A lady is in prison here, who on being admitted to see her husband, a convict, changed clothes with him to allow him to escape. They are both in prison now. What sad stories one hears every day—'Every one to his own way!'

"The weather has now turned fine. Davidson will probably have reached Irkutsk by this time. We may possibly meet him on his return journey, if he does not await our arrival.

"We have seen the Governor, who was most friendly. He will do his best, in both the cases we mentioned. He also gave me his card to secure horses without delay at the posting-stations. At 6 p.m. our tarantass with droika will be ready. God bless you, my darling! may His presence go before us on the way!"

Telegram from Krasnojarsk, July 17. "Ebenezer!"

"Irkutsk, Thursday, July 17.—You would have been greatly amused if you had seen us last night, after our arrival in this hotel about 10 p.m., enjoy a well-cooked cutlet with salad and potatoes. Oh, it was a feast, after such a weary journey from post-station to station, with never a hot meal. Our dietary on the way consisted of tea and eggs and dry black bread in the morning, then a quart of milk and bread about 2 p.m., and tea, bread, and sardines in the evening. We were thankful when-the fresh horses were ready to take us on, and could not bear that the time should be wasted.

"Nature is ever fresh and new. The country is really in many parts very pretty. The flowers of the field were a never-ceasing object of admiration. I often wished you were with me to enjoy the rich abundance of the loveliness around. Many flowers that would be considered choice in Europe's gardens, here grow wild; and the hills, and the forests!

"We arrived here all safe and well, praise the Lord! This morning I had such a feast of your dear letters. Mr. Davidson will return to-morrow to his home in Ekaterinburg. He has been a great help to me with the books. They have given him much anxiety and trouble. Now, I have them all here, thank God, and we can go on with our work. Dear Kargel has been most helpful in arranging for horses at every post-station, day and night. He very quietly got out of the tarantass at each stopping-place, so that I might be as little disturbed as possible. Some of the stations are 15 verst apart; others are 30 verst. The horses drive from 10 to 12 verst an hour; so he never had any continued rest. I am very thankful for his help in every way. So, under such favourable circumstances, I have travelled this long journey, and at the end of it I am well and in excellent spirits for the Master's further demands.

"At Alexandrowskaja, 70 verst from here, there is a large central prison with about 2300 convicts. This prison also we hope to visit. Davidson is going there with us on his way back, though it is somewhat out of his route.

"On the way between Krasnojarsk and here we had the opportunity to visit an etape prison, and spoke to 225 men, and gave books. To Kargel and me it was like a brook in the desert. For while travelling one has to be occupied so much with one's self, food, comfort, etc. etc. Twice we had to put our tarantass into the wheelwright's hands. There are generally breakdowns on the way; and we have fared better than most travellers.

"This place, Irkutsk, was burnt down some years since. It has not recovered its former greatness. There are many good houses and shops, but many buildings are still in ruins. It is said that the standard of morality is low. What can be expected, where sin is rampant and the gospel withheld?"

"*Friday, July 18.*—I have called on the Governor this morning. We have just sent off packages of books to Chita, beyond Lake Baikal, to await our arrival. Oh, praise the Lord! His mercy endureth for ever! All is well with me! Our God has His eyes on us for good. He has appointed us to fulfil His purposes of mercy. Praise Him! All the way, through miles and miles of the loneliest forest conceivable, we have not seen a single wild beast, nor any evil-disposed human being. The nights are intensely cold, and the days very hot, yet by day and by night He has kept us under the shadow of His wings, I have not lacked any good thing in any way. Praise Him evermore!"

"*Sunday, July 20.*—We went to Alexandrowskaja large prison, leaving here on Friday at 10 p.m. and arriving there about 8 a.m. yesterday. There were 2500 prisoners. With great readiness we were taken by the officials right into the heat of the battlefield for

God. We were allowed quite as much liberty as we might have had in England in the streets. Indeed, we had more. Everything was arranged for us by the officers in charge, and so we had open-air meetings of prisoners, and proclaimed the gospel to them freely and fully. In the evening 400 or 500 men returned from work. We had them drawn up in a square, and Kargel and I, standing on the cart in which our books were, spoke to them all, the officers also listening most attentively, and several of them being deeply moved.

"We had a whole day of it. The chief took us to his house to luncheon. When we had finished, we drove back to the posting-station, and left for Irkutsk at 11 p.m., and arrived here all safe and well about nine this morning. It was a happy, full day, and we felt delightfully tired after it.

<table>
<tr><td align="center">SCRIPTURE TESTIMONY</td></tr>
<tr><td align="center">A sower went out to sow seed,
and some bore much fruit

MATTHEW 13:20-23 · MARK 4:3-9
· MARK 4:14-20 · LUKE 8:4-15</td></tr>
</table>

"I found some cheering traces of former gospel testimony. A young man from Dorpat, who had heard me preach there several years ago, was present.

He was a student; and working in a chemical laboratory had procured some prussic acid, by means of which another man had committed a murder, for which he had been condemned to Siberia. This young man was sentenced to six years imprisonment, and exile. He has been in prison already four years. His joy was great when he saw us. Strange to say, he and the Christian Jew whom I saw at Krasnoyarsk had been for some time together in prison, and both knowing me had talked together of what they had heard through my preaching in different places. It is very humbling to see how the 'bread cast upon the waters' returns 'after many days.' The Lord be praised for these tokens of His favour!

"I received telegram to-day, saying, *'Weston-super-Mare tele-graphs* HALLELUJAH.'

"We have had a full day, visiting the prisons here in Irkutsk, and have not quite finished. Shall go again tomorrow morning. We saw to-day two political prisoners, women. They were apparently quiet people. There were some dissenters in the prison whose case is under examination. They are Christians, in bonds for the truth's sake. They were arrested for speaking against pictures and icons (images). May God have mercy on their accusers!

"One man wept with joy when we gave him a New Testament. He had borrowed one from a fellow-prisoner, but now his great wish was fulfilled; he possessed the book he longed for. Sad and painful are many of the stories we hear; but the sufferers who suffer wrongfully, have the victory nevertheless. A large proportion of the convicts are unable to read. Great numbers of them are hardened in sin. A baroness who murdered her husband and then married a lackey, talked as if she were a Christian. It was nothing but empty Lutheranism. Many such criminals call themselves 'politicals' in order to gain sympathy. It is not easy always to discern truth from falsehood. The boy we released from the prison in Tomsk, we have restored to his mother. May God in His mercy magnify the power of His grace, and bring forth abundant fruit from the gospel seed that we sow among the prisoners. We again saw several boy prisoners; one, an accomplished pickpocket. The time that they spend in confinement with other criminals is a certain advance for them towards utter destruction. Yet no provision is made for their isolation.

"At last we have left Irkutsk behind us. The Governor kindly gave me a 'billet,' which ensures our obtaining post-horses, where otherwise we should have to wait for many hours, as other travellers are obliged to do. Three post-stations along the road we come to the Baikal lakeside. The steamer will carry our tarantass across. Travelling in tarantass is not at all unpleasant where the roads are tolerably level. One cannot undress, of course. My leather coat is a great comfort to me, and over it my thin overcoat. When it turns cold I have my Berlin coat at hand. The fur coat is safely packed as yet. I have told you, the books are the ballast of our conveyance and the substratum of our seats. The portmanteaus rest in the front of the carriage, and on the top of this luggage we manage to lie down and sleep during our journey. The Siberian post-horses run at a great speed: the drivers urging them on at a furious rate, only by talking and shouting to them.

"Hitherto, indeed, we have been marvellously helped. Praise Him!"

Lake Baikal, to Stretensk (about 1000 miles) by Tarantass

"We arrived at Lake Baikal late at night. At five the next morning we went aboard, and arrived at the other side after about seven hours' passage. It was cloudy; the mountains in the neighbourhood of the lake were hidden, and there was little to see except the deep dark waters.

"On board we met with a Russian priest who, with his family, is on the way to Kamtschatka. They came from St. Petersburg, and he is sent as a missionary. We gave him forty of our New Testaments, for which he was most grateful. He seems to be a real Christian.

"Two Jewish merchants who travelled with us some of the way to Irkutsk, and then went on in front of us to cross the Baikal, met with a sad accident. They had their tarantass fully packed with goods. On board the Baikal steamer, one of them, being very tired, lay down in the tarantass on top of his goods and fell asleep. When the boat started and met the sea, she began to roll so strongly that the sleeping merchant was thrown out of his conveyance, and fell into the sea. Before help could be rendered

he was drowned. His companion, his clerk, had the painful duty
of conveying the sad news to his wife and seven children. He
appeared to be a friendly man, and Kargel had some profitable
conversation with him. He accepted from us gratefully the Psalms
of David. Death is in the midst of life! But to us, life is in the
midst of death! Glory be to the Lamb!"

Telegram from Chita, July 29, "Ebenezer!"

"Chita, Wednesday, July 30.—Here we are all safe and well. We
arrived yesterday about 5 p.m., exactly five days after we left
Irkutsk, having travelled without much intermission all the time.
This is the place where Baron Rosea and his fellow-exiles, the
Dekabrists, were sent. The population is about 4000, chiefly
exiles and their descendants.

"This is really the beginning of the prison district. There is a small
prison here, but we shall probably leave this to-morrow for
Nertschinsk, where the silver mines are, with gangs of convicts
at work in them.

"The scenery between the lake and here is really most beautiful, especially on the Selinga River. The world of flowers we saw
would have charmed you. Every day we seemed to espy new specimens; one amongst many was the edelweiss, and many Alpine
flowers in their deep tone of colour. It was an intense delight to
me to see them, and I several times made the driver stop while I
gathered some rare blooms, but, alas! they soon faded.

"We had some amusing encounters on the way. Last Sunday we
stopped at a Buriat (Mongolian) village. The head servant at the
post-station was a converted Buriat, and through him we had the
entrance into several Buriat jurtas. He translated our conversation
with them, I speaking German, Kargel translating into Russ, and

the Buriat into Mongolese. We had a good time there. We also joined you and the Church of God in remembering the Lord's death in the breaking of bread. We then started again eastward.

"At Berchneldinsk we visited the large new prison. Last night we called on a doctor Alexieff, whose wife is English. They have asked us to dine with them to-day at two. She gave me an English cake, which is a treat. We have just seen the vice-governor, and were received very cordially. The Governor is away. He invited us to accompany him to the prison at six. There are but few prisoners here. We hope to-morrow to go farther, to Nertschinsk, the real centre of the convict prisons, where we shall be relieved of our burden of books. Nertschinsk is 267 verst from this, and we shall be two days on the road, I expect.

"This is one of the most elevated towns in Siberia. It lies away in a valley, high among the mountains, 4000 feet above sea-level. All provisions must be carted up either from east or west at enormous expense. No corn can be grown here.

"Our hotel is a very primitive place indeed. It is far behind as to accommodation, and only to the front in the prices they charge. However, we take such things with good humour. Beds? Nowhere! We have a limp, emaciated mattress spread feebly upon hard boards. I am very thankful for my air mattress, and for the sheets and towels, as nothing in the way of bed-linen or pillows is supplied.

"The Buriats gave us some of their tea to taste. They boil the tea in milk. It looks like soup, and is insipid, and not particularly clean."

"*Nertschinsk, Sunday, August 3.*—We arrived here yesterday at about 5 p.m., ordered dinner at the hotel, and went at once to the prison to learn what number of men were there. We then returned, had some refreshing warm soup and a cutlet, and again visited the prison and had a good time. It is not large, only about 105 men. The premises are in a very tumble-down condition; they are about to rebuild.

"We have now reached the very centre of the Siberian convict-prison system. Within a radius of perhaps 500 or 600 verst lie Akatui, Algatschi, Pakrowski, Zerentui, Alexandrowski Zavod, and Kara. Here, then, is our programme for this week. We have a great number of books to be taken to these prisons, and we may have difficulties in procuring sufficient horses to carry them from place to place. We shall have quite a caravan for some days, one tarantass, and two covered carts laden with the books. But we are of good comfort, for He has sent us, and He is with us Who never fails with His ready help in time of need.

"We shall to-day join you and the whole family of God in remembering the Lord's death.

"I am very thankful for this day here in Nertschinsk. The scenery we passed through is lovely; very wild in some parts; over tremendous rocky mountains; and in such solitude, rarely a human being to be seen. The floral world is magnificent. It is like a vast garden. Flowers, the most lovely deep blue, the golden yellow, and others deep pink or violet, abound in rich profusion everywhere. The forests are silent. Scarcely a bird is to be seen or heard, and no animal makes its appearance; but God is everywhere to be seen in His marvellous works.

"We are now on the eastern slope of the Appletree mountains, and the water-courses run towards the Pacific Ocean. The population consists of Mongols, Tunguses, and Buriats; there are also some Chinese.

"All the officials, high and low, are very pleased to help forward our work; and in the prisons we have unlimited liberty to speak the gospel. The priests do not make their appearance. At one large prison the priest did appear when we arrived, and suggested that all our books should be placed in the library! We did not agree to this; so he made himself scarce, and we saw him no more.

"We have had such a restful night that we feel quite fresh for a new start. May our Blessed Lord keep your heart in perfect peace! 'He is our Peace.' My love to all the Lord's children."

"Stretensk, Tuesday, August 5.—Here we are on the pier of the Amoor steamboat; but we have yet to visit the prisons in the mining district and Kame before we can go on board the vessel. We hope on August 22 to start for the voyage to the mouth of the river on the east coast.

"We spent Sunday at Nertschinsk and then came on here in our tarantass, with the two carts following close behind us. It is a weary time for me to be without news from you. It is a trial of faith and patience. How great my longing is just to have a glimpse of you, and Harry, and Emmie, I must not tell."

"Wednesday, August 6.—We have decided to visit the mines, travelling in our own conveyance, and then to return to this place. This is a busy town just now. Travellers coming every day have to wait for the steamer. This hotel is close to the pier. Horses are to be here at eight o'clock to-morrow morning. I must therefore prepare for the journey. The tarantass is to be packed with our books. This is no trifle, as we have to take about one thousand of them with us. The loads require to be rearranged after every prison visit; and now we have the care of the cases sent on in advance from Tkutsk. Some we shall send on ahead down the Ampor River, and the remainder we hope to dispose of in the prisons and mines."

Telegram, Stretensk, August 16, "Ebenezer!"

"Stretensk, Saturday, August 16.—We returned safe and well this morning from our expedition in the mountains and mines among the hard-labour criminals. Our tarantass has done the work well. We are thankful that we took it; and in it the books for the different stations. We could never have stood the travelling in

Convict Chained to Wheelbarrow

a post-cart. The roads were rough in some places. We were very thankful when we were able to lighten our conveyance of some of the packages at the first prison-station, which we reached after thirty-six hours travelling, sleeping in the tarantass.

"The first prison is Alexandrowskaja Zavod. The second is Algatschi. The third is Kutamara, where there is a smelting furnace. The fourth is Kadaya, where we entered a silver mine. The fifth is Gomi Zerentui, the largest prison of all. The sixth is Malzawskaja Rodnik. The seventh is Nertschinskaja Zavod.

"We had happy work, unlimited liberty to preach to and converse with the men and women, some of whom were deeply moved. In none of these prisons had there ever been Bibles or Testaments given before. They were very thankfully received, and the officers were most kind. Nothing could exceed their kindness. I am so thankful to God that we have been able to visit these places. No one has ever been there to show an interest in the prisoners, most of whom are hardened criminals, murderers, etc.

"It is a sad sight to see so many men and women unable to take care of themselves, whom it is necessary to watch and guard to keep them from injuring their fellowmen. They are not in chains, except a few of the most desperate. One man was chained to a wheelbarrow. His was a special case. Some of the criminals work in the silver mines; but their labour is by no means harder than that of an ordinary workman. They work eight hours a day. In the smelting furnace they work twelve hours. Their treatment is not hard nor cruel. They are well fed and clothed, and after a period of good conduct they arc allowed liberty to live in their own houses and to work for themselves. They are then under daily roll-call control

"The mines are close to the Manchurian frontier. It is very mountainous, and quite uninhabited, except these penal settle-ments. When they have served their time they live in the village which is attached to the prison. It is a sad sight to see the people of these districts. There is rarely a smile on any face. They listened most attentively to our addresses. Several men wept. Many expressed gratitude. Some fell on their faces and thanked God. We have at last found a corner of the earth where the gospel has never in any shape been heard. There are, including Kara, 10,000 men and women criminals in these places. Some of the prison buildings are very bad; but new ones are in course of erection. Altogether, the prison department in these parts is in very good hands now, whatever it may have, been formerly.

"The scenery is very wild—high bleak mountains and deep valleys and gorges stretching for vast distances in absolute solitude. The meadows and hillsides are covered with most beautiful flowers. On some hillsides wild peonies abound much as we cultivate in our garden, and many other magnificent flowers.

"The frontier of China is only 8 to 10 verst away at some points. Some prisoners make their escape; but they are usually recaptured, and have their terms lengthened; or they perish by the way, as there is not a living soul to succour them. If they cross the frontier, the Chinese arrest and beat them, and deliver them up to the Russian authorities.

"The Director of Prisons received us most kindly, and facilitated our seeing everything. The Governor in Chita had given him notice of our arrival. On entering the prison at Gorni Zerentui, I found that two men were confined in the dark cell for special discipline. At my request they were at once released. We went down a silver mine by the shaft-ladders and saw the ore in its native veins. The officers pointed out the work the convicts had to do. Each man is given a certain amount of labour, which, if he is industrious, he can finish in about six hours. If he is idle, it will take him eight hours or longer. From all I have now seen, I have a right to discredit many evil reports about the Siberian prisons. In a few days we shall hope to see the politicals also, at Kara.

"I am sorely tried in being deprived of the joy and comfort

of your letters. I think of you constantly; and of Harry and of Emmie, who I trust will be strengthened in purpose and made meet for the Master's use. God bless you, and make you a blessing more and more, my darling wife! Kargel is very helpful in many ways. I have been kept in excellent health, praise God! and have not wanted any good thing all the time. Travelling through a country inhabited by a criminal population, we have never seen an evil countenance turned against us, nor any wild animal, nor has any accident happened to us. Not a hair of our head has been harmed, praise our Heavenly Father!"

"Sunday, August 17.—God grant us to rejoice in the communion of saints!"

"Thursday, August 21.—We have been to Kara, and there reached the climax of the Siberian prisons. The worst criminals are kept there, men and women who even profess to have forgotten home and name and everything of the past. Is it possible? They certainly are designated by a word which in English would mean 'Know-nothing' or 'Having forgotten everything.' We also saw the 'politicals.' In one prison were men who were Revolutionists; in another, eight women. They are educated and clever people. One of the ladies has already been ten years here. They have many books to read, and have the privilege of writing. They cook, and do all the necessary housework. But they were very nervous and excitable; they have gone through so much suffering. We heard at Kara the whole story of the lady who was flogged with the plet. She was a desperate character.

"The officers have a rough time with the 'politicals.' We offered the New Testament to them; the men said they had Bibles, and only one accepted a copy. The women all accepted New Testaments gratefully, and we had some profitable conversation with them.

"To Uz Kara we travelled by boat and went to Nijni Kara (15 verst) with post-horses. The work in the prisons is most cheering. The poor creatures are so grateful for the word spoken; and many of the officers equally so. They say, if our prisoners could hear such addresses only two or three times a year it would make a great difference. Their priests practically do nothing for them. They are left to themselves, and to the powers of evil in and around them. A man in Uz Kara wept sore. He owned that he deserved his punishment. His wife and family live in London. He begged very hard that I should visit them on my return. A poor German pleaded with tears for a German New Testament, which we were not able to give him, all the books of other than the Russian language being already spent. He was able, however, to read Russ, and we gave him a Russ copy.

"I am weary for letters from you, my darling wife; but must exercise patience. Had I known more of Siberian travel I might have given you different addresses to write to; on the way, instead of cutting off my hope of letters from you until I reach Japan. After several times prayerfully considering the question whether we might return to Europe by land, we have come to the conclusion that this would be almost impossible. Winter and ice set in September. The only way open will be by sea from Japan. I shall never leave you again for so long a time, or go so great a distance. However, I am not like Jonah. My Lord is with me here, and is preparing every step of the way, as He has already done. I have been marvellously helped.

"We have sold our tarantass for 80 roubles. The first bid made for it was 75 roubles. A great number of conveyances are here for sale. They are bought up by Jews, then cleaned, repaired, and painted, so that they look like new, and then re-sold. It seems hard to dispose of the dear old thing in such an unfeeling way, yet this is its lot. It has done us good service. Besides carrying us, it has been loaded with many hundreds of books. We have got attached to the conveyance in which we have been made to feel our bones very often, but in which also we have had much joy and comfort, much praise and prayer. In the mining district I do not see how we could possibly have done without it; it was our house and all"

Stretensk to Saghalien (about 1800 miles) by Steamers

"Pahrowka, on board steamer, Tuesday, August 26.—We are at last on the river Shilka. A telegram from Capt. Etholén in St. Petersburg secured us a free passage to Nikolajewsk. Of course we pay for all our food. This is a very great boon, for we shall be a fortnight going down the river. I made Capt. Etholén's acquaintance at Helsingfors. He is one of the directors of the Steamboat Company. A cabin was at once secured for us, and we receive every attention. It will be an easy but wearisome journey. Our cabin we have to ourselves, which gives us opportunity for reading and prayer, and for writing.

"To-morrow we are to meet a steamer coming up, by which I hope to post this letter. The river Shilka is very shallow in some places, and navigation is difficult. We hope to enter the Amoor to-morrow, where the waters will be deeper, as it receives the Argun, which flows from the heart of Mongolia. We came on board yesterday at 6 p.m. The food is good; and the hot regular meals are a great luxury after our mode of living on our journeyings by tarantass. The samovar was the great consoler at all times, and eggs and black bread; but one gets very tired of this after a while. However, I am learning to be in want and abound, and the Lord supplies all our needs very richly. I am writing in my cabin, the map on my knees. The steamer shakes rather, and the ink does not flow freely. My warmest love."

"Blagowestschensk, Thursday, August 28.—We arrived here yesterday afternoon. We found we must change steamers, so at once transferred our goods and chattels to the boat lying alongside.

"After arriving here, we went to call on a Dane to whom I had an introduction from the Governor of Chita. There we found the address of a merchant in whose house meetings are held, and very soon, to our great surprise and joy, we found ourselves in the midst of loving brethren. The people here are Molokans. Many of them have been converted and baptized. A meeting was arranged at once, and we had a refreshing season.

"To-day we are to call on the Governor, visit the prison, dine at 2 p.m. with M. Paulsen the Dane, have supper at 7 p.m. with the Molokan merchant, and then we are to have a meeting. To-morrow morning at ten, the steamer leaves.

"This is a rising place. Established only in 1854, it now has upwards of 20,000 inhabitants. A gold mine in the neighbourhood has attracted a population. The name of the town means "Resurrection." The first man I spoke to yesterday, the agent of the steamboat company, spoke English! The Amoor is a fine stream of water. It marks the boundary between Russia and Mongolia. For four days I have had China on my right and Russia on my left, and my prayers have been much for China, and also for Russia. Across the river is Aigun, a Mongolian town.

"The scenery on both banks of the Amoor is very striking; but both countries are very sparsely peopled. We saw oil dozing out from high rocks in one place. The vegetation is different from what we have seen previously: oak trees with very fine and beautifully cut leaves, and Siberian apple-trees with fruit as small as a hazel-nut.

"My thoughts are much with Emmie, who will soon go forth into the Lord's harvest-field and reap for Him in China. May God graciously accept our offering, and bless our dear child!

"This country is very fine; and the people enjoy more liberty than in Russia. There are great resources here which have not been touched. Many Chinese make themselves useful in various ways, and are valued as workmen. The mighty stream of the Amoor is full of fish, and the scenery in many parts grand and wild; men are very few and far between.

"Leaving Blagowestschensk, we crossed the river and landed at the Chinese town Aigun, where we had the opportunity of seeing real Chinese life. The people stared at us. My beard attracted their notice and admiration. We looked into several houses, and saw one of their temples. Some men admiring my beard, one of them asked my age. When I told him, I asked his age. To my amazement he told me 'Twenty!' He looked quite old and withered, and was an opium-smoker. The people appear generally good-natured and contented.

"At Khabarovsk, the Government town, I called on the Governor, to whom I had letters of introduction. Then we visited the prisons, so filling up the time of waiting. We again changed our steamer here. Most of our fellow travellers here turned south to Vladivostock, while we go to the north, still travelling on the Amoor River, which spreads out like an arm of the sea, and enters the sea at Nicolajewsk, about 400 miles farther on,"

Telegram from Nicolajewsk, September 5, "Ebenezer!"

"*Nicolajewsk, Friday, September 5.*—The Lord brought us here in health and safety yesterday afternoon by the Amoor steamer *Alexei*. We had every attention and comfort on board owing to Capt. Etholén's kind telegram. And now we have long and weary time of waiting in front of us, until the steamer *Baikal* is ready to take us to Saghalien, and this will not be until 18th September. This will make us later at Tokio, and so much longer without news from home. What this costs me, I cannot tell you. On arriving here we were perplexed what to do. There is neither hotel nor boarding-house in the town. The police-master, and the agent, to whom I had letters, did not offer to do anything; but an American merchant kindly offered us hospitality in his house, and to him we are going to-morrow morning. There is a post three times a month. The cases of books that have been sent here to me from Odessa, will just be in time to supply the Saghalien prisons. I am very thankful to have been enabled to undertake this journey, and that you were willing to let me go to do this service for our Lord. Surely you will be a full sharer in the spoil!"

"Nicolajewsk, Sunday, September 7.—This is the Land's End of Great Russia. Siberia is a fine country, and by its fertility might rival any land, if only a population were found to cultivate its broad acres and to farm its magnificent meadows; to fell the thousands of square miles of dense forests, and to dig in the earth for its precious metals, The day may yet come, in God's providence, when the millions of overcrowded Europe may migrate eastwards, just as now they do westwards

"The journey through the continent of Asia, from the Ural Mountains to the Pacific Ocean, would have great charms for the tourist or the scientist; but to us every step of the way was taken charged with blessed responsibility; since all along the way there are exiles and captives, souls who have the first claim on the gospel of 'deliverance to them that are bound.' The interest increased, and was intensifed with our progress; but it reached its climax in the mining district of Nertschinsk and of Kara amongst the hard-labour convicts and the political prisoners and exiles. I have had the inestimable privilege and honour of distributing on this journey about 12,000 copies of the Word of God, and of preaching His gospel to upwards of 40,000 prisoners."

"On board steamer nearing Yokohama.—God has indeed marvellously guided and provided. On Thursday, 11th September, we left Nicolajewsk to cross the Gulf of Tartary to Saghalien; at 5 a.m. on the 13th we arrived. As the steamer was taking coal we had a good time for the Alexandrowskaja prison. The Governor of the island resides there. We were afterwards conveyed by a small steamer to Port Dué. We distributed several hundreds of scriptures to the prisoners, and preached the gospel to them. What books we had left we gave into the care of the officers, who promised to give them to new arrivals at the prisons on the island. Thus we were taken to Saghalien against everybody's expectation (the outbreak of cholera at Vladivostock having caused serious interruption of the very occasional summer communication between Nicolajewsk and the island). Also sufficient time was given us there for our work, and then in the night we passed on to Hakodate in Japan. For these two further proofs of our Father's loving guidance and care of us, as for all the remarkable interpositions of His good providence with which this journey has been crowded, we praise His Glorious Name! Hallelujah!"

Telegram from Tokio, September 23, "Ebenezer!"

Here the extracts from the letters must cease; not because the interest abates, but because the places hereafter visited are the scenes of more or less familiar Christian work. We have hitherto followed the evangelist in a spiritually pathless wild. He sowed and he reaped on virgin soil.

From Tokio he passed on to Yokohama. He had hardly set foot in the city before he was recognised and claimed as an old friend by

View of Convict Settlement, Akatui

one who had heard him preach in New York. He also dined with the Russian consul, Prince Lebanoff. A Spaniard and an American were his fellow-guests; and as the consul's wife was a Greek, the party was international.

Along the Pacific he sped to Shanghai, where he spent two days; thence to Hong Kong, from which island he paid a flying visit to Canton; thence to Saigon and Singapore. Here he gave several public addresses in the Town Hall, and in the open air to the Chinese by interpreter, and visited the prisons (of course), preaching by interpreter. He spent a fortnight in Singapore, busy all the time for the Master. Then he resumed his homeward journey; and travelling *viâ* Colombo and Port Said, reached England in the beginning of December.

CHAPTER XIII

In Finland and Scandinavia

TO write the story of Dr. Baedeker in Finland is to tell of the earlier years of the work of the Baroness Mathilda von Wrede, whose picture [follows] this page. To her was given the honour of taking the doctor inside the gates of a Finnish prison for the first time. That first visit was made to the prison at Helsingfors on the 3rd June 1887. On his subsequent visits the young Baroness was his faithful helper

> **SCRIPTURE TESTIMONY**
>
> *Jesus came for sinners and those rejected by society*
>
> MATTHEW 8:1-13 · MATTHEW 26:6 · LUKE 5:30 · LUKE 7:34

and interpreter. Her influence in the prisons is still a great blessing; for she has consecrated her gifts and her life to the service.

University professors frequently interpreted for the doctor. On one occasion when a professor was translating, the convicts stood in their ranks respectfully listening, a set, stony look upon their faces. It was plain that they were quite unmoved. On his next visit to the same place the doctor was accompanied by the Baroness. He had not proceeded far with his address before the moist eyes of the listeners, and the convulsive twitching of their features, told him that the "arrows were sharp in the heart of the King's enemies."

"How was it?" he afterwards inquired wonderingly of one of the officers in attendance. "My former appeal they heard with indifference, and even resentment. Today the Word has found their consciences and hearts. Where lay the difference?"

The prison-officer's, reply was significant:

"The difference, sir, was in the translation. When you said 'My beloved friends,' or 'My brothers,' your clever professor invariably translated the expressions 'men,' 'prisoners.' But the young lady translated it into Finnish as you expressed it in German: 'My beloved friends,' and 'My brothers.' The key that opened their hearts was human compassion and affection. They are not used to it."

The Baroness von Wrede is the daughter of a former Governor of the Wasa Province. When quite a girl, her heart and life were surrendered to Christ, and sanctified by His Spirit. She began to seek for souls in the convict prisons of Finland when about nineteen years of age, her father's high position giving her access to places to which ordinary persons would have been curtly denied admission. For years her influence for good among the convicted criminal classes of Finland has been extraordinary. In her early womanhood she appeared to be the victim of a rapid decline, and the doctors gave but little hope that her life could be saved. Her father was in an agony of grief.

"O Matilda!" he cried, "what can I do to save you? Will you not try to get well again? Will you arouse and determine to recover if I promise to give you a house, an institute, for your prisoners' mission?"

"Yes, dear father," she replied, her eyes sparkling brightly at the prospect. "Indeed, I will. God helping me, I will be strong again."

She made a good recovery, and gained the house for her prisoners; and, in addition, a considerable extent of land. For her overjoyed father, as a thank-offering, made over to her one of his estates in Finland. The place was prepared for the reception of discharged prisoners who gave signs of sincere penitence and a genuine desire for reformation. One

Baroness Von Wrede

of her brothers (a man like-minded with herself) took the oversight of this humane and Christian enterprise.

On one occasion the Baroness, calling at a prison on her customary visitation, was informed that a particularly violent and ferocious criminal was in his cell awaiting trial and punishment. He was charged with the commission of no fewer than eighteen murders, some of them being of peculiar atrocity.

"Let me see him," she begged of the Governor.

The Governor smiled pityingly upon her.

"My dear child, I could not think of such a thing."

"But I must see him. God can save even such as he! Where is his cell?"

It was not difficult to discover the cell, for there were several armed warders on guard outside the heavy door.

"Open, and let me go in!" she demanded.

"I really dare not let you risk your life. It is far too unsafe. He is almost a maniac!" said the alarmed Governor.

However, the young Christian worker declared she was willing to take all risk, and insisted on gaining admittance to the cell; so with great reluctance, and many protests, they yielded.

"Please do not touch the little slide in the door to peep in; nor interrupt us while I am in there!" was her parting request to the little group of amazed officials who stood in the corridor. Then the warder turned his key and withdrew the bolts, and cautiously opening the door a little way, the heroine glided inside.

A slight rattle of chains directed her attention to the object of her search, stretched at full length upon his hard bench. He was a huge, massive giant of a man. Quickly she walked to where he lay, and stooped slightly over him.

"Are you awake?" she inquired.

The murderer gave a sudden start, as if electrified. It was almost a leap bodily into the air; and his heavy irons clanked loudly as he fell back upon the bench,

"I have come to see you," she said gently.

There was no answer.

"Won't you talk to me?"

"Who are you?" he inquired fiercely.

"I am a friend. I want to be kind to you, and to help you."

"Who sent you here?"

"I have come of my own wish, for your sake."

"I could kill you—with one blow! Get out of my cell!" he cried hoarsely, and his chains rattled again with the violence of his passion.

> **SCRIPTURE TESTIMONY**
>
> *Jesus will never send away those who come to Him*
>
> JOHN 6:37

"But you won't kill me," she replied, with a silvery little laugh. "That would not be any use. I want to do you good, not harm—to speak to you about the Lord Jesus."

"Go away, I tell you! I will not listen." Again the rattling links, as the ruffian put up his hands to his ears.

"Then I shall pray for you at home; and I shall come to see you again soon. We all need forgiveness; and when I pray, I will ask God to forgive you as well as myself. Good-bye!"

The prisoner made no reply, and she left the cell as quietly as she had entered. Again and again the Baroness visited that criminal, and gently pleaded with his seared and deadened conscience.

"I want to know who you are?" he asked, on one occasion, curiosity overcoming his petulance.

"I am the daughter of Baron von Wrede," she replied. The prisoner stared at her.

"You never mean to tell me that a morsel like you are the daughter of that fine handsome man!" he exclaimed.

"Of course I am," she said. "We cannot all be tall and handsome like my father *and you!*"

At this pleasant compliment his hostility completely collapsed. He was silent for a minute or two.

"It is not the least use your talking to me," he resumed.

"Nobody can do me any good. My heart is a rock!"

"How glad I am to hear you say that!" she answered brightly.

"What do you mean?" he inquired angrily.

"I am glad your heart is a rock," she explained; "for I have seen flowers, yes, and sometimes even trees growing from the rock, and so have you. A tiny seed falls into a crevice in the side of the rock, and takes root, and grows, and covers the rock with beauty. So I hope some word the Lord will give me for you, may take root in your rocky heart, and grow. I am praying that it may be so."

And it was so. Her prayers were answered. That cruel unmanageable murderer became a changed man. God gave her that soul. His ferocity left him. With deep penitence he took his awful crimes to Him who said, "I will in no wise reject him that comes."

> "Lions and beasts of savage name,
> Put on the nature of the lamb."

By way of contrast I transcribe the following, from one of the doctor's letters to England:

"I have written to the Baroness von Wrede about making another tour of the prisons in Finland with her. Did I tell you that in one of the prisons at Abo, where I spoke to about 400 men, many of them imprisoned for life, the Director of the prison was quite overcome, and before all the prisoners he thanked me with tears in his eyes, and I embraced and kissed him in the sight of all the men and officers and guards? God be praised for His unspeakable gift, and for the free gospel both to governors and to criminals!"

Dr. Baedeker took an enthusiastic interest in Finland, and here he frequently declared his message of grace. In the days when Finland groaned and writhed under the heel of despotism—days that we hope have passed for ever—the evangelist brought home heart-moving stories of the condition of affairs in that land. The women made it a practice to attend all meetings—his own included—dressed in deep mourning for the sorrows of their country. General Bobrikoff's rule excited sore apprehension on the part of the Finns for their ancient rights. The new proposals in regard to military service, among other matters, filled them with dismay. I can hear the impassioned prayer of the veteran as he led us at the throne of grace, in our little prayer-meeting in his drawing-room: "O God of the seventy-second Psalm, deliver the needy when he crieth, and the poor and him that hath no helper! Spare the poor and needy; redeem their soul from Violence; for precious is their blood in Thy sight."

A letter written by the doctor from Reval contains this sentence: "I pine after the prisons in Finland." He had a quenchless heart-hunger in him for the souls of men. What a picture this is, in a letter written from St. Petersburg:

"I arrived here last night from Finland, where I had the joy of preaching to many prisoners; first at Helsingfors, then at Tavast-ehus, Abo, and Wilmanstrand. It was a sight to melt one's heart to see 300 to 400 men, usually prisoners for life, and to see their eager faces, all intensely interested in what was said to them. The Baroness von Wrede translated for me. She is the only person who has an entrance into the prisons. I take it as a great favour from the Lord that she introduced me into these strongholds of the law. It was a sight not easily forgotten—strong, fine men with intelligent faces, bound in heavy chains."

Dr. Baedeker's visits to Helsingfors University were always appreciated; his addresses to the professors and students being attended with much blessing. Indeed, an entire chapter might be written on his work among students. This must, however, suffice:

"Helsingfors.—On arrival here the time was at once mapped out; and we have had happy meetings every day. At our meeting yesterday I spoke in English, one brother interpreting into Swedish, the other into Finnish. The hall was full, and for two and a half hours the interest was maintained. Some professors of the University are coming out, receiving with meekness the engrafted word. Praise God! Dear Baroness von Wrede was with me this morning. She evidently overtaxes her strength. But she is so bright and happy in her work. She would not for anything in the world draw back in the least degree. Take care of herself, she simply cannot. Oh, it is good to be in His keeping, for His service!"

The spiritual atmosphere both in Finland and in Sweden was greatly to his mind. In both countries he had many most attached friends among the nobility. There was always an eager bidding as to which should enjoy the honour and privilege of entertaining him on his visits. It was a choice refreshment to his spirit to enjoy fellowship with these brethren and sisters in the Lord, who, notwithstanding, those almost insuperable barriers to entrance in at the strait gate, noble birth and high rank, were rich in faith and heirs of the heavenly Kingdom.

Just a glimpse or two of his *Stockholm* work:

"This morning I had a drawing-room meeting with one of the ladies of the Court; and afterwards I called on the Princess Royal, who received me most kindly, and showed a warm interest in evangelising work in Russia. She promised to pray for me. Now I am come to stop with Mr. B., and I have had to write to Baroness von F. that I cannot go to them. It is a long journey by rail, and my time is very full here, praise God! Count S. has given me some letters to different governors. The trouble will be to find it in one's heart to leave the places. I have invitations from Baron S. to go to his son's country place, and from Baron U. to go to him, and now from Baron von H. to go to them. I shall need heavenly wisdom to say 'Yes' and 'No.' I know you pray for me, and many others likewise, and this is a great comfort to me. Although hitherto the Lord has put open doors before me, I can only rejoice with fear. I need His guidance from day to day, and from place to place. Yesterday the Lord gave His messages with much power, and He laid hold on some souls.

"There is One at the right hand of God always pleading, on our behalf, His precious blood, shed once for all. His arms have no need of being propped up with stones under them, for He never wearies. We poor mortals are so forgetful, and soon tired out."

Here is an extract from another *Stockholm* letter:

"I leave by the steamer *Tornea* this evening for Finland. I am very thankful for the time the Lord has given me here. I had an interview with the Princess E. and, to my great surprise, the Queen, who is slowly recovering from an illness, sent for me. I had the honour of speaking to her for about half an hour. Many souls have been helped and set free for service. The Lord has made the way and given the word, and I cannot be too thankful for the glorious time in Stockholm."

Dr. Baedeker's ministry was like his Master's, in this respect— he was never off duty. Like the Chief Shepherd, he went out after the *one* that was lost, eager to bring it back at any cost.

> **SCRIPTURE TESTIMONY**
>
> *Gospel is the power of God for salvation*
>
> ROMANS 1:16

He was one day travelling in Sweden. Opposite to him in the railway carriage sat a young Swedish lady. He invited her to accept a tract. She did so, and thanked him pleasantly, telling him at the same time that it had no interest for her.

"Why not?" he inquired.

"To be frank, I am an unbeliever—an agnostic," she replied.

"I am sorry to hear it. I trust, however, you will read the little booklet, and think about it. It may be that God in His great mercy will open your eyes."

This appeared to her like a challenge to an intellectual battle; and being well furnished both for defence and attack, she straightway took up the gauntlet. But she did not know her interlocutor. The weapons of his warfare were not carnal, but mighty. They were not upon a common plane of thought or of life. She was puzzled; and her heart was irresistibly warmed towards this stranger, so obviously sincere, so interested in her highest welfare, so in love with the things of God—a Being whose very existence she had come to doubt—so concerned about her soul.

"I believe the Lord will yet lead you to Himself," said the doctor. "He is seeking His wandering one, and will find you in the end."

"I am not at all sanguine as to my conversion," she laughingly replied. "There are so many questions I should require answers to, first."

"Will you make me a promise?" he pleaded.

"What is it?"

"That when God does convince you of sin, and lead you to Jesus, you will write to me, and let me know?"

"Of course I will promise that, if you would like me to. It will not be yet awhile. To whom and where shall I send?"

"Here is my card, and I shall pray on till your letter arrives."

That letter took eight years in coming; but it came, and was duly delivered at the doctor's home in Weston-super-Mare. The lady was, in more recent years, the guest of Dr. and Mrs. Baedeker. She has been for years past an earnest and prominent worker among young women in Sweden; the one bitter regret of her heart being that in her past life she had been so terribly zealous in the dissemination of her baneful sceptical ideas. This is the story of Miss Alma Nesbeth.

To his labours in Norway space will only permit the barest reference. The doctor, at the advanced age of seventy-eight, writes thus from *Christiania:*

"You would be glad if you could see the great crowds filling the halls where I am privileged to tell out the wondrous story of Jesus and His love. I have had the prisons opened to me; the head-warder and the chaplain being both true believers. We began by doing what the Holy Ghost tells us to do, 'Greet one another with an holy kiss' (2 Corinthians 13:12), and our hearts were on fire for the poor criminals.

"My days are running out, but the dear Norwegians have the art of filling in the precious hours, and my God has never failed to give strength. To-morrow, after the last meeting-in the largest hall, holding several thousand people, I hope to depart by night-train for Göteborg, where I am to be till Monday morning; thence I go to Jönköping, where the people are looking for large assemblies, many believers being in the place, and where I hope to be till Friday. On Saturday and Sunday I am expected at Sköfde; on the 20th I return to Stockholm, and on the 21st by steamer to Finland. The lights on the lampstand were so arranged as to throw all their light upon the Light-bearer, 'Who walketh in the midst.' 'Not unto us, O Lord, but unto Thy name give glory!'"

CHAPTER XIV

Beside the Caspian Sea

MR. BRYCE exhibits a piece of wood which he discovered, and detached with his ice-axe, among the virgin snows that cover the upper slopes of Mount Ararat. He claims (with a sly wink) that there is stronger evidence that it is an authentic relic of the Flood than can be produced for many other relics that are preserved in many places with the utmost veneration.

"I am willing to submit it to the inspection of the curious," he declares. Anyhow, it will be hard to prove that it is not 'gopher wood.'" [1]

Mrs. Baedeker also possesses a trophy from Ararat, brought to England by her husband on his return from one of his many visits to Transcaucasia. It is a fragment of rock. There can be no reasonable doubt that it was under water during the Flood. It is therefore, equally with Mr. Bryce's timber, a venerable memento of a great event, or at the least of an interesting locality.

Of the doctor's evangelising journeys in the vicinity of Ararat, we have frequent accounts in his letters. He delighted greatly in his labours for Christ in Transcaucasia. It was a country not easy to reach; by the

---

1   *Transcaucasia and Ararat.* By the Right Hon. James Bryce, p. 280.

most direct route it took a week's travel from St. Petersburg. Many
languages were spoken by the inhabitants. It is still the land of Babel
of the human race. Facilities for travel among these wild rugged mountains that thrust their summits up into the eternal snows, were prac-tically nonexistent. Comparatively recently, travellers

> **SCRIPTURE TESTIMONY**
>
> *True disciples love Jesus more*
> *than even their own lives*
>
> MATTHEW 8:18-22 · MATTHEW 16:21-
> 28 · LUKE 9:57-62 · LUKE 14:25-35

have complained that it was impossible to secure in the winter season
a warm and clean shelter at night. There are wild animals in abundance
in these well-nigh inaccessible solitudes: wolves, lynxes, herds of wild
swine, leopards, and wild cats; though they never appear to have
troubled Dr. Baedeker. But still more dangerous, the mountain roads—
or tracks—were infested with Kurdish, Persian, and Tartar brigands.
In 1900 a converted Georgian monk in the employ of the British and
Foreign Bible Society, went out from Tiflis to visit among the mountain
villages, and never returned. It was thought that he had been murdered
in some lonely pass. Even last year (1906) it was stated that highway-
men were terrorising the railway officials along the main line, and that
in Erivan, only the central parts of the town could be regarded as
safe—and safe only during daylight!

But all this was as nothing to our dauntless apostle. Were there not
beloved exiles in banishment to visit and cheer? And were there not
also the charmingly artless and affectionate communities of Armenian
Christians to nourish with the Word of God, and to cherish in the
faith?

Let us accompany Dr. Baedeker in one of his many tours in that
historic land.

After a busy and eventful voyage down the magnificent river Volga
from Nijni Novgorod, calling at the towns on the banks and visiting the prisons, the doctor, with his companion-interpreter Count
Scherbini, arrived at *Astrakan* on the Volga delta, situated among the

CASPIAN SEA
RUSSIA
R.Volga
Astrakhan
Petrovsk
Derbend
Baku
Shemakha
DAGHESTAN
CAUCASUS MTS
Mozdok
Vladikavkaz
Mt Elbruz
Kasbek
Tiflis
GEORGIA
Elizabetopol
R.Kur
Aletzandropol
Kars
L.Gokcha
Erivan
Shusha
Mt.Ararat
L.Van
ARMENIA
Erzerum
ARAS R
SOUTH RUSSIA
R.Manytch
R.Don
Rostov
Taganrog
Sea of Azof
CIRCASSIA
R.Kuban
Stavropol
CRIMEA
Simferopol
Sevastopol
Kherson
Odessa
Kishinev
R.Dnieper
BLACK SEA
Sinope
Trebizond
Batum
Poti
Kutais
TURKEY IN ASIA
British Miles
0 50 100 200 300
50°
40°
30°
E.M.L.

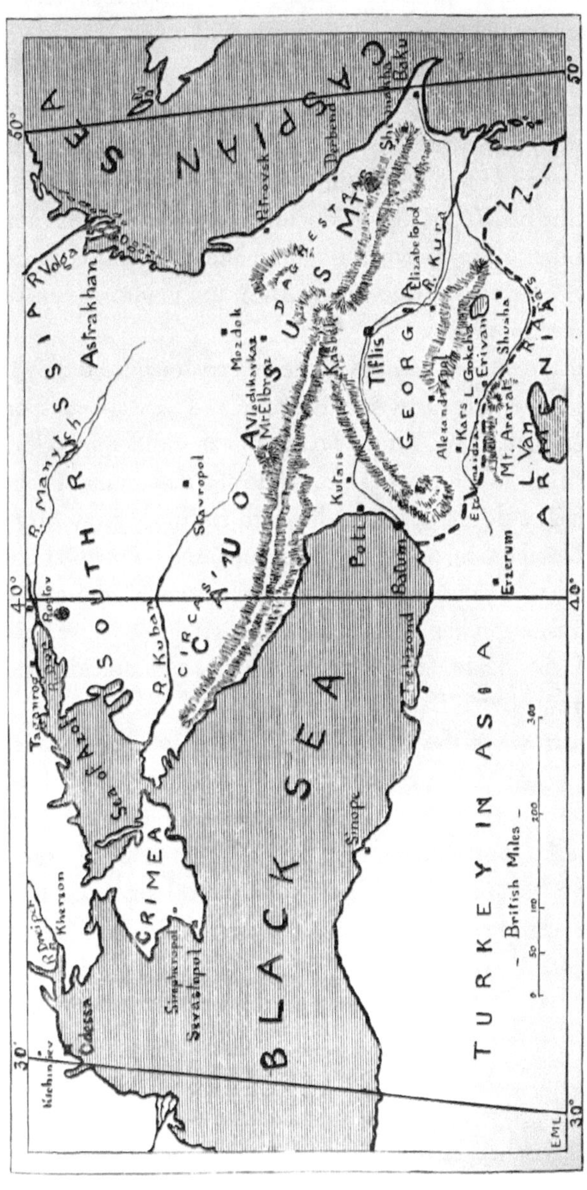

Caucasia

immense flat swamps that fringe the north Caspian shore. Here they embarked for Baku, a voyage of nearly 500 miles.

The mouths of the Volga River, where it empties into the Caspian Sea, are considerably silted up, and embarkation is troublesome. A small sailing vessel of light draught takes passengers and cargo over the shallows and past the sandbanks, to the Baku vessel that lies out beyond the bar. To his joy the doctor discovered that the captain and several other officers were Finlanders; and, in addition to their own language, could speak Russian, Swedish, and English. They were most agreeable shipmates.

The first night was stormy and the sea very rough, and the passengers were glad when they arrived at Petrofsk, and were able to spend a day in shelter there. The Count, who was but an indifferent sailor, begged the doctor to forfeit the tickets and do the remainder of the journey by land. The doctor was not disposed to throw away fifty roubles and undertake a three days' driving tour, and so they "abode in the ship." The next morning, the wind having somewhat moderated, the captain made another venture, and although the waves were still rather agitated, they had a fairly pleasant voyage, and landed in delightful summer weather at Baku.

The sorrows of the women and children on board touched the doctor's heart, as always. In the rough weather, and with the water breaking over the ship, their condition was pitiable. He ordered a good meal of hot soup and bread to be given to all and sundry; and when they had enjoyed the meal, and the colour had come back to their pale cheeks, he told them of the love of the Lord Jesus.

He was always received with demonstrations of affection by his Armenian friends in Baku.

The Count and he went first to an hotel; but the Armenians would not hear of their remaining there. They must come and

> **SCRIPTURE TESTIMONY**
>
> *Christians are generous*
> *and hospitable*
>
> ACTS 16:14-15 · ROMANS 12:13 ·
> I TIMOTHY 3:2 · HEBREWS 13:2

abide with one of their number, as their guests. To adapt himself to the ways of an Armenian household, or any other, long practice had made easy to the doctor. This was not quite the case with the Count, but He got on fairly well

"They showed me much love and gratitude," said Dr. Baedeker, in describing his visit. "As I entered the house, the dear wife met me at the door with a basin, and poured water over my hands, and then gave me a towel."

"Our house belongs to the Lord Jesus," said his Armenian host and hostess. "Therefore regard it as your dwelling-place whenever you come to Baku."

"The hospitality of these dear people is boundless," said the doctor afterwards. "I felt utterly ashamed. We may teach them from the Word; but they act the Word, and leave us far behind."

Then came the meetings. The Armenian congregation in the city was without a preacher just then, as the pastor was away ill. So he had a free course. They began on the day of arrival with a meeting at 4 p.m., and then a "good warm" prayer-meeting at 7 o'clock. At the latter meeting an unusual incident occurred, an outward demonstration of hearts overjoyed at the visit of their spiritual father. A lady had come prepared to honour their teacher and visitor by washing his feet; but he protested, and refused to submit to this, and the basin and towel were reluctantly removed.

At another meeting two ladies and a gentleman sat in the front seat, and at the close spoke to him in English. They had heard him preach, years before in St. Petersburg.

"This is pleasant," said the doctor to them, with his irresistible smile, "but of no real profit unless you have found the Lord!"

Baku, the city of oil wells, is a flourishing place, peopled by all nations, but quite Asiatic in character—Turks, Tartars, Persians, and Armenians, who wear their ragged clothing with an air of noble self-importance. The streets are crowded with sellers of fruit and all kinds of things. There is a running rush and hurry, and people tumble up against each other most ludicrously. Dr. Baedeker thought they were a very elastic sort of people, falling soft, and soon on their feet again. The houses are built in a square, a garden in the middle of the square, and rooms and outhouses around.

"In England," said he to his host, "our houses are built in the garden; but your garden is in the house!"

The Armenians are the mercantile class of Baku, and many of them are wealthy. He found them virgin soil for the gospel; and he considered that the Tartars would be reached and evangelised most effectually through them. The women are too much kept in subjection. He arranged some Bible-readings for women; and they came in great numbers. They sent greetings to Madame Baedeker, and begged the doctor to ask her to come and teach them. He was not sure that she would be able to bear with some of their domestic habits and arrangements if she came. But he did not tell them so. To them, everything was as it ought to be; and the doctor fell in with their ways as "to the manner born," much to the delight of his hospitable friends.

There are no trees in Baku; and the streets, on dusty days, are oiled, not watered; but the water is lacking to flush the streets and sewers, and fevers make havoc. The doctor admired the "fine asses" trotting about the streets, and the silent lumbering camels; also the abundance of fruit exposed for sale: pomegranates—the rind coarse and unsightly, the inside delicious—and splendid grapes, all very cheap.

The dress of the women deserves description. A broad ribbon is worn over their mouth, and fastened round their neck with a broad silver chain. A silk handkerchief is also worn over the head, hiding the forehead, so that it is practically impossible to see the face. Their robes are usually trimmed with fur. In the meetings they sit cross-legged upon the floor like the men, behind a wooden partition; or in another apartment, where they may listen unseen.

In the neighbourhood of Baku there are great numbers of Molokans, the Quakers of Russia. The term "Molokan" means, literally, "milk person." They have been the subjects of severely repressive measures under the Government for their religion. They do not practise baptism nor celebrate the Lord's Supper, nor have they a regular ministry. Their lives are simple, and their characters above reproach. Many of them are well-to-do. They welcomed the visits of Dr. Baedeker. At one of their meetings, while the doctor was in the midst of his address, the proceedings were interrupted by the appearance of a police-officer, He ordered the meeting to cease, and demanded that the doctor and Count Scherbini should follow him. They went as directed to the police office; but Dr. Baedeker sent a message to the Governor of Baku, which had the effect of securing their immediate release; and they returned to the anxious assembly of Molokans and resumed the address.

From Baku to Schucha by road is a long and tedious journey. Schucha is in the neighbourhood of Mount Ararat, "the father of mountains," snow-capped, that towers above the great plain on which it stands, nearly 15,000 feet. On the peak of Little Ararat (the smaller of the twin mountains) the boundaries of three Empires meet— Russia, Persia, and Turkey. The robbers who infest the Armenian mountains, when sought by the arm of the law of one country, dodge over the frontier into another. The Russian territory is *supposed to be* the safest.

Dr. Baedeker joined company with a Russian Government official, in a tarantass and troika for the journey, and found him a considerate travelling companion. Count Scherbini had gone on to Tiflis to visit some friends. They had to stop a night on the way, at one of the rough roadside post-stations where horses are changed. They slept on the floor. The Russian had brought a bed with him, and very kindly lent the doctor his heavy Caucasian coat to wrap around him. Fatigue and exhaustion induced sleep. The next day they met several caravans of Tartars coming down from the mountains to the plains for the winter. They return to the colder latitudes in the spring. It was quite patri-archal, the droves of cattle, horses, donkeys, and sheep. The women and children were riding on the backs of horses and donkeys. Even the cows had to carry their appointed loads; and the fowls, perched on the animals' backs, appeared to enjoy their ride as much as the humans. The doctor thought of patriarchal and pastoral scenes in the book of Genesis—of Abraham and Lot, of Laban and Jacob—as they threaded their way among the patient flocks and herds.

Schucha is on the high road to Persia from Tiflis. The road runs south across the wide plain, 50 miles or more in width, that separates the two Caucasian ranges. Its nearest railway station is Ewlach, on the Baku-Tiflis line, about 75 miles away. The town is inhabited by Armenians, Tartars, Persians, Turks, and a few Russians. There is a population of about 40,000. It was the scene of the faithful labours for Christ of Count Zaremba, afterwards banished. Fruit of his holy ministry is yet to be found. There are many earnest Christians among the Armenians. By them Dr. Baedeker was welcomed as the messenger of God.

"I, have great entrance with these people. They drink in the Word eagerly, as the parched ground drinks in the dew."

A local Armenian brother who could speak German, Russian, Armenian, and Turkish, was his principal interpreter, giving his services freely and gladly for love of the gospel. As, however, some of the Russians attended the meetings, the services of a second interpreter also, into Russ, were necessary here.

At Schemacha also, Dr. Baedeker found an eagerly opened door. This mountain town, the scene of a calamitous earthquake in 1902, is near Baku. The journeys to these places, over the high mountain passes, partly on horseback, partly by the Russian droshky with post-horses, were not without hardship and danger. But God ever preserved him. When the Armenian Christians received news of his approach, they came out to meet him, some in conveyances, and many afoot; and he entered the place in a kind of triumphal procession. The results of his evangelistic meetings in these towns were extraordinary. The people pressed by scores and hundreds into light and liberty. In one mountain village near Schemacha, when at the close of his address the doctor appealed for such as desired to be converted to God, and to be disciples of the Lord Jesus, to stand up, the entire congregation started to their feet and gazed at each other and then at the doctor in astonishment. Presently one of their number broke the perplexing silence.

"Yes, of course, doctor. That is why we sent for you! That is just what we have come here for!"

Mrs. R. C. Morgan sent home to England from the Caucasus, on the occasion of the tour which she and her husband made with Dr. Baedeker, a series of deeply interesting descriptive letters. I am glad to quote her narrative of the visit to Baku and Tiflis.

"Baku, the oil city, a forest of pumping engines!

"What a dreary approach! Naphtha everywhere, filling the holes of the bad roads, forming little ponds, floating on the surface of the seawater-reservoirs and inlets. A little girl comes along with a bucket which she fills with this mixture, and there is a poor, ragged man, carrying two buckets full, which the poor people try to make a living by selling.

"The air, like the soil, seems to be impregnated with paraffin. For many miles around nothing but desert. Every blade of grass seems to have a hard struggle for existence; but men will come and settle down, bear with hardships, and defy the climate, for the sake of gain.

"Almost every European nation has its consul in Baku.

"We remained in Baku for a week, holding meetings every day. On the Sunday Dr. Baedeker and Mr. Morgan addressed four gatherings—Armenians morning and evening, and Russians and Germans in the afternoon. The running thought was that neither baptism, nor the Lord's Supper, nor conformity to certain rules of worship, nor profession of any kind, could make of a sinner a saint; only living faith in Jesus, and an entire separation from the world unto the Lord with singleness of purpose, could effect the manifestation of a Christian life, and make us meet for the Master's use.

"We left Baku on the Friday night, after a farewell meeting, at which Dr. Baedeker referred to his first coming fifteen years ago.

Several of those present were the fruit of his first labours. Tears were in their eyes as they took leave of their spiritual father. Was it for the last time? Would they see him again?

"Two women cried piteously as they prayed for the conversion of their families. One of them had the joy of seeing her grown-up son promise to walk henceforth with God; the other, at the close of the meeting, said to us, with tears still glistening upon her cheeks: 'It was I who thrust my children into the world because I was worldly. Now that I am converted, it is my duty to pray them out of it.'

"After the dreary surroundings of Baku, Tiflis, the capital of the Caucasus, with its picturesque situation on the river Kura, was a delightful change. Some say that its beauty is superior to that of the Alps. Others, that though grand and wild, and rich in glaciers, it is poor in rivers, waterfalls, and lakes. Its white-capped giants, Kasbek and Elbrus, both claim the honour of having had Prometheus chained to their rocks. It is the rocky home of classical myth.

"Explorers have a hard work in this region. Besides the paucity of roads, there is the immense barrier of language. Far beyond the reach of modem communications live the remnants of old nations, some of whom many centuries ago have sought refuge in its precipices from the destroying hand of their persecutors. Some, like the inhabitants of the Daghestan Mountains, are divided into many tribes, each shut up to a valley, or a single village, unable to understand their neighbours. To say that twenty different languages are spoken in the Caucasus is well within the mark. It cost Russia sixty years of warfare to subdue these mountain races, the greater proportion of whom are Moslems. Handsome types are among them, especially the Tcherkess men; also the Grusians, who have a tradition that they are older than the Egyptians. Tiflis was the capital of their kingdom from the fifth century.

"Here, as in Baku, we were heartily welcomed and kindly entertained by friends of various nationalities. One Christian brother, a business man in the town, and of German nationality, had been banished for eight years, first to one place for making propaganda among the Russians, and then to another for having divided money among Stundists, sent to him for that purpose. 'But the last place was the best,' he added. 'I found many friends there, and willing ears for the Gospel.'

"Meetings took place at the Russian Baptist Church and at the Swedish Mission House. At the last one, a woman who had come in with her-daughter unawares, broke down under a strong conviction of sin, professing to yield her heart to God."

"'Oh, how I love these dear Tartars, Persians, Armenians, Tcherkess, Grusians, and so on,' Dr. Baedeker would say. He loved to pass through the Oriental bazaars for the sake of human study.

"'Oh to touch these hearts with the power of the gospel; to make vibrate the silent chords of Divine love in their souls which would transform their lives. What a privilege to him who accomplishes it!' This was about the gist of his talks, generally ending with: 'If I were a young man, I would set to learning Grusian at once.'

"More than once we were asked with regard to our friend, 'Is he paid for what he does?' and our answer, 'No, he does it for Christ's sake,' generally met with an astonished look, and the final remark, 'Then he must be a really good man.'

"In a prison on the shore of the Caspian Sea we were met by the priest, who was the chaplain of the prison, and, who greeted Dr. Baedeker very warmly, having known him on previous visits. He was evidently deeply interested, and went through the prison with us for two or three hours, listening to the words spoken, and seeing the books given and received, his eyes sparkling, though sometimes dim with the moisture of unshed tears. He told Dr. Baedeker that when he himself gave a book to a prisoner, he remembered the sweet wolds he had heard from him. The priests of the Greek Church do not preach, nor have they much, if any, opportunity to hear preaching. This may explain the delight with which one who loved the Lord listened to the simple declaration of the gospel of Christ, the power of God unto salvation to every one that believes."

Dr. Baedeker's worst foe in the Caucasus was fever. It sadly crippled his energies, although even it could not subdue his intrepid soul. It is pathetic to read how he was frequently aroused from sleep, and brought from his sickbed to conduct a meeting at which an eager audience was anxiously awaiting his arrival; and then returned to bed to snatch a few hours feverish rest, if possible, before the time for the next meeting came round. These fevers greatly depressed him. Oh, how he longed at these times for a brief sight of England and home!

With an extract from one of the letters, this chapter must close.

"*Batoum.*—The enemy has had much to say to me during this last week. First the difficulties and delays on the road. Then the blocking up of the road to Erivan and Kars. Then when I returned to Tiflis, the fever! It appears to me that the power and influences of evil are gaining ground in hindering the gospel. I had a vision last night of all the horrible devices of the enemy, how he places obstacles in the way of the gospel reaching the ears and hearts of sinners; how he deceives the people into thinking that darkness is light and light is darkness. If ever I preach again, I must preach against sin!

"I have sadly missed your letters lately. The mountain roads are blocked up with snow. You cannot think how lonely I feel at times, without anyone to speak to, or to pray with, or to give me a little sympathy. I often have a great longing to be with you. Oh, how I miss you! I find out now what a sorry missionary I really am. Perhaps I was too old to begin such a mission to the prisoners. It is such an enormous field, and I have only touched the margin of it. I may but do what l can while I live, and leave the rest for others. I cast it all on the loving Father, Who knows all, and Who knows His poor feeble servant, who is not fit to be left alone. To-day's texts greatly cheer and help me.

"The Mohammedans are calling for prayer from their minarets; the nominal Christians are eager after business and money."

CHAPTER XV

"And Others were tortured"

IN the city of Vienna, in the year 1892, George Müller, at the age of eighty-six, laid his hands on the head of Dr. Baedeker, then a comparative youth of only sixty-eight summers, and "separated him to the special ministry to the banished brethren, committing him to the loving care of our Heavenly Father."

What a scene for an artist!

That there was need for someone to pity them and to help them is manifest. The Holy Orthodox Church of Russia had resolved that Stundists and all other dissenters must be sternly dealt with.

In August 1891, M. Pobiedonostzeff called a great Conference in Moscow, of Orthodox ecclesiastics from all the forty-one Russian episcopates, to consider the burning question of the best methods of preventing the spread of sectarianism in the Empire. Great alarm was expressed at the rapid growth of the Baptist, Stundist, and "Paschkoffist" heresies. Statistics were presented to the delegates proving that twenty-eight out of the forty-one dioceses were badly "infected;" and that "the virulence of the infection" was such that it was entirely beyond the control of the clergy. One of the delegates declared that under the stress of persecution, a few Protestants were returning to the fold; but, alas! they were exactly those persons whom the Protestant communities were too glad to get rid of.

"What are we to do," he asked, "to win back to our midst those earnest and God-fearing men who have left us, and despise us?"

The answer of Pobiedonostzeff to this searching question—as embodied in the resolutions finally adopted by the Conference—was a determination to employ severer measures of repression.

"The rapid increase of these sects is a serious danger to the State. Let all sectarians be forbidden to leave their own villages.... Let all offenders against the faith be tried, not by a jury, but by ecclesiastical judges. Let their passports be marked, so that they shall be neither employed nor harboured, and residence in Russia shall become impossible for them. Let them be held to be legally incapable of renting, purchasing, or holding real property. Let their children be removed from their control, and educated in the orthodox faith."

These were a few of the practical measures of repression adopted. The following specimens of Pobiedonostzeff's Penal Code give a vivid and painful insight into the sufferings of these faithful and patient children of God, of whom the world was not worthy:

Article 187.—Offence: Leaving the Church for another religious community. Punishment: Loss of civil and personal rights. Transportation. In milder cases eighteen months in a reformatory.

Article 189.—Offence: Preaching or writing religious works to pervert others. Punishment: First offence, the loss off certain personal rights, and imprisonment from eight to sixteen months. Second offence, imprisonment in a fortress from thirty-two to forty-eight months. Third offence, banishment.

Article 196.—Offence: Spreading the views of heretics or dissenters, or aiding such. Punishment: Banishment to Siberia, Transcaucasia, or other remote part of the Empire.

Try to imagine the experiences of two of the brethren on whom the heavy hand of orthodoxy fell, as described by themselves. When arrested they were "taken to a police office and stripped of their clothing. A heap of discarded prison clothes lying in a corner was pointed out to them. An officer ordered them to select and put on whatever clothes would fit them. The garments were horribly dirty, stained with filth, crawling with vermin, and utterly abominable."

On the march, after the day's exhausting journey, "the footsore prisoners were herded together in small and unventilated rooms, with absolutely no arrangements made either for comfort or decency. In one room, twenty feet by fifteen feet, no fewer than sixty of them passed the suffocating hours of a summer night."

"We will make them conform, or we will harry them out of the land," said that "high and mighty Prince James Stuart" to the British Nonconformists of his reign. An Archbishop of the Greek Church circulated in Russia a number of leaflets that breathed out similar threatenings and slaughter. One was entitled "The damned Stundist." Here is a sample of its verses (for it is, save the mark, a "poem"!):

> "Boom ye church thunders!
> Flash forth ye curses of the councils!
> Crush with eternal anathemas,
> The outcast race of Stundists!
>
> "Dark and gloomy, demon-like,
> He shims the flock, the Orthodox,
> He skulks in nooks and corners dark,
> God's foe, the damned Stundist."

Pretty, isn't it? The sentiment is so humane, so noble, so worthy!

In the "nooks and corners dark" Dr. Baedeker, like a ministering angel of God, sought out these poor, hunted-down and chained human beings to pour in the oil and the wine of sympathy and succour.

"These suffering saints are usually transported with the other prisoners, and often in chains, until they arrive at their destination. They are then set free to settle down in a district appointed for them, under strict police supervision. In some of the places to which they are sent, it is next to impossible to find a living. At a Tartar town in a remote corner of Transcaucasia, I found many banished brethren quite destitute. One fortunate brother, a good penman, had found a situation in an office, for which he was paid five roubles (ten shillings) a month. He had a family of seven, who occupied one room, in which another family also lived with them. The relief I was able to give them, drew forth a flood of grateful tears.

"The number of exiles sent over the Caucasus has lately been greatly increased. They are mostly Stundists, Molokans, and Baptists: men and Women who have been taught by the Word of God, and who will not bow in worship to pictures, nor receive absolution from priests. In Transcaucasia they are set at liberty, and land is sometimes allotted to them for cultivation. They generally construct for themselves a hut made of earth and covered with turf and branches.

"Thus Russia treats her best citizens; and these men are real heroes of patient endurance.

"At Tiflis we went to one of the large prisons which I have visited before. They are mostly all new prisoners; those of last year being sent farther on. Three brethren were brought in in chains. One of them recognised me, and wept sore. Their homes and wives and children are in the neighbourhood of Moscow. It is cruel work! These are the Czar's choicest subjects. We were cautioned not to have much intercourse with them. But the shake of the hand and the brotherly embrace, were good cheer to the dear exiles.

"We visited (his interpreter and he) the prisoners at Baku, Elizabetpol, and Tiflis, and had again the joy of giving relief to a number of brethren, who with their families were on the way to exile. At Tiflis we met seven brethren with their families, together twenty-seven souls, in the prison. A grandmother was among them, who told us that this was the eleventh prison through which she had had to pass! They were to go to Elizabetpol, and there they would be told in what place they must spend the next five or more years under the most difficult circumstances, and yet closely watched by the police. The number of police is legion, and their zeal is excited by the rewards held out.

"A sister whose husband has been in exile nearly three years, received a police visit about 5 a.m. A loud knock at her door demanded entrance. Fifteen policemen entered. The chief officer made apologies to her while the others carefully searched through wardrobes and cupboards, etc. Of course, nothing was found that could incriminate her. The same night other persons had their repose disturbed for the same purpose. All papers, accounts, letters, etc., were carried away, and will not be restored for a long time. Such searchings are in most cases preliminary to arrests.

"At *Elizabetpol* (on another occasion) I found in the prison quite a number of *Dukobors,* a sect who seek to live by obedience to the Word of God, but who seek salvation through obedience. They were a fine set of men, strong and joyous in their sufferings, but they find no favour with the authorities, and will probably be exiled for life to the island of Saghalien. They eagerly listened to words spoken to them, and most grateful were they for the New Testaments.

"At *Gerüsi,* a far-away place hidden among the mountains, we saw most of the brethren in that desolate place of banishment. The journey to it is very dangerous, especially at night, partly because of the road, which mostly runs alongside very deep abysses, and partly because of violent robberies, which are frequent.

"One could not help thinking how differently we should have felt if we had been sent as banished ones along these wild and dangerous mountain-tracks. The joy of the brethren in seeing us, and ours in meeting them, was a great feast, short but sweet

"The brethren here meet in each other's rooms and sing and pray together."

"*St. Petersburg.*—The news from the Caucasus is most sad. Some of the brethren who had been banished for five years, and were brightly looking forward to their release, have been ordered to remain an additional five years 'because their original term does not appear to have changed them!'"

"*Moscow.*—At Baku I had again the honour of being closely watched by a police officer. Being suspected has a very depressing effect on one's spirits, and I have learned to sympathise with our brethren in banishment. For their sakes I was obliged to be cautious in my movements. I can ho longer move about freely and unobserved as formerly. Even my visits to the prisons were under special surveillance, and an officer travelled with me until I was safely beyond his Government boundary. It was a real rest to get away, and to have ten days' happy gospel work with the German colonists in South Russia."

The ecclesiastical and civil authorities were not the only persecutors of the Stundist. The mob rose up against him: and a man's foes were they of his own household. One of his proteges, who had learned the way of salvation from a man-servant in the employ of the vice-governor of the province, told the doctor his pathetic story. It will serve as a sample of many. This poor refugee to Roumania had a hard time of it before he finally succeeded in making his escape. His wife being very-zealous in her newly found faith, destroyed the icons (the holy pictures) with which her house was adorned. When the village got to hear of this act of desecration, the neighbours, accompanied by their own relatives, stormed the house, and so severely maltreated the pair that they left them unconscious. That was the beginning of many months of suffering. His brother, being the village elder, and of great authority, seized his possessions, live stock, and even clothing. The windows and doors of his dwelling were broken; his freehold land was taken and let to a tenant, the rent being payable to the coffers of the church. When he went to a higher authority, this dignitary told him to go and "take the cholera!"

> **SCRIPTURE TESTIMONY**
>
> *A man's foes will be those of his own household*
>
> MATTHEW 10:34-39 · MATTHEW 12:48-50 · LUKE 8:19-21 · LUKE 9:59 · LUKE 12:49-53
>
> *Believers will suffer terrible things for the sake of Jesus' name*
>
> MATTHEW 24:9-14

After a few months of this, with starvation threatening his family, he appeared before the village council to beg them to grant him a passport that he might leave the district. For answer, he was seized, bound hands and feet together, and hung thus from a ceiling-beam. Then they tortured him with needles and hot irons, until his screams caused them to-cut the ropes, when he fell heavily to the floor upon his head. This outrage brought on an illness which it is a wonder he survived.

When he had recovered, so malicious and persistent were his neighbours, that on Sundays and festival days he was obliged to leave the village early, and spend the day in hiding behind the hedges to avoid them. Then came a visit from three priests to examine him. The visit not being satisfactory, although he said as little as possible, he was put into the local prison. The next day two gendarmes came, and by the direction of his brother the Elder, he was taken to the blacksmith's forge. He was there ordered to curse his faith; and when he refused, his hand was put in the vice, which was screwed up tightly. Then with a heated iron his hand was burnt—there were twelve scars upon it.

Silently in his agony he looked into his brother's face. Said his brother: "The devil is in you, but I will drive him out!" Then they proceeded to apply the hot iron to different parts of his body; and when they were tired of torturing him, he was taken back to prison.

While there he was informed that he had been condemned to be sent to Siberia. He decided to make a desperate attempt to escape. In the dead of night he broke a window of his prison, and succeeded in getting free. Running swiftly to his home, he awakened his wife, and taking the youngest child, they fled. Hiding by day and tramping in the darkness, they came by the goodness of God to Elizabethgrad, where they knew some brethren in Christ. These helped them, and passed them on to other friends until they arrived at Odessa, whence they escaped to Roumania and to comparative safety. This brother, like many others, found a true friend in Dr. Baedeker.

Enough has been written to show the nature of the service rendered by the doctor to the Church and to the Master, in this field. How thankful we all are that the iron yoke is now in measure removed from the necks of the children of God in Russia.

CHAPTER XVI

Dr. Baedeker and Count Leo Tolstoy

THE profound interest excited in Russia by the ministry of Dr. Baedeker is reflected in contemporary-Russian literature. As an instance we will take one of the novels of Count Leo Tolstoy, Resurrection,[1] a work which describes in detail Russian prison life, a nauseous and revolting picture.

"Kiezewetter" and the "Englishman" two distinct characters in this novel, are manifestly sketches of one and the same personality—Dr. Baedeker.

Kiezewetter is a foreign preacher, who "for about eight years" had been discoursing on Redemption in the stately ballrooms and drawing-rooms of the nobility in St. Petersburg. Tolstoy describes him as "the German," although his address was delivered in English—a significant coincidence. The other character, the "Englishman," is an erratic traveller, who distributes New Testaments, and evangelises in the loathsome kameras of the Siberian prisons.

Count Tolstoy is decidedly hostile in his treatment of both characters; for what reason, one is unable to divine.

---

1   Resurrection. By Count Leo Tolstoy, translated by Mrs. Louise Maude.

"A footman entered the apartment where the countess was conversing with the prince, her nephew, and presented a note on a silver platter.

"'It is from Aline,' said the countess. 'Now you will have a chance of hearing Kiezewetter!'

"'Who is Kiezewetter?' the prince inquires.

"'Kiezewetter? Come this evening and you will find out who he is. He speaks in such a way that the most hardened criminals sink on their knees, and weep, and repent.'"

This appears to fix the identity of the character. He is an evangelist who is accustomed to preach both to aristocrats and to hardened criminals. I think it is perfectly safe to assert that Dr. Baedeker was the only English speaking German who combined these two widely different ministries, evangelising in the palaces and in the prisons of Russia.

One would imagine that a preacher who merited such a tribute as the above, to his success amongst the most depraved and desperate classes, was worthy of better treatment at the hands of the novelist, than sneers and travesty. But Tolstoy wishes to set forth certain economic ideas; and there is no room in the novel for praise of any other gospel.

"'Aline has a wonderful Home, the Magdalen Home,' the countess continued. 'I went there once. They are terribly disgusting. After that, I washed and washed. But Aline is devoted to it, body and soul.... If your Magdalen could hear Kiezewetter she would be converted. Do stay at home to-night. You will hear him. He is a wonderful man. We shall have some prayers afterwards.'

"'It does not interest me, *ma tante*,' replied the prince."

This young man, Prince Nehlúdof, poses in the novel as a social reformer; yet the Divine message that is able to bring hardened criminals to their knees, to subdue Magdalens and convert them, and to cause noble ladies to abandon lives of selfish luxury in order to give themselves, "body and soul," to the Christlike mission of rescuing their "terribly disgusting" fallen sisters, has no interest for him! Prince Nehlúdof displays extraordinary bigotry!

Count Tolstoy's picture of one of these aristocratic gospel meetings, which he regarded as a mere fashionable craze, is interesting. It was held in the evening after dinner, at the residence of the Countess, in the large ballroom.

> "The high-backed carved chairs were arranged in rows. Beside a little table on which stood a Carafe and glass, an armchair was placed for the preacher.
>
> "Elegant equipages stopped at the front entrance. The great room, richly furnished, filled with people. Ladies were there in silks and velvets and lace, with false hair, and laced-in and padded figures; and among them were men in uniform, and evening-dress, and some five common people, two men-servants, a shopkeeper, a footman, and a coachman.
>
> "Kiezewetter spoke in English, and a thin young girl, wearing a pince-nez, translated into Russian, promptly and well."

The address as distorted by the novelist does not deserve notice, except for one particular. The preacher in this palace of princes is apparently as unsparing in his denunciation of sin, and in his condemnation of self-complacent, luxurious, perfumed sinners, as his Master would have been. The message to these purple-blooded children of affluence and authority is, "Flee from the wrath to come!"

This also, one would have thought, would have won Tolstoy's approval. But no! He is no more pleased with Kiezewetter's message than he is with that of the "Englishman" to the Siberian prisoners, "Tell them that Christ pities them!"

"Sobs were heard in the room. The countess sat with her elbows on an inlaid table, leaning her head on her hands.... A senator's daughter, a fashionably dressed girl, knelt with her face in her hands...."

It is greatly to be regretted that the novelist considered it desirable to turn this scene into coarse burlesque. It is written, "He that turneth many to righteousness shall shine as the stars for ever and ever."

"The Master praises: what are men!"

Let us take the other character, the "Englishman," who appears in the end of the work. He is travelling in Siberia for pleasure, visiting the prisons, preaching to the convicts, and circulating copies of the Scriptures among them.

At the date of the writing of the novel (1894) the doctor had just completed his second great visitation of the prisons of Eastern Siberia, returning to Europe by Singapore and Suez. Dr. Baedeker was the only Englishman who held a universal and unrestricted permit to visit Russian prisons in Europe and Siberia; and, I suppose, no other foreigner is ever likely to enjoy such a privilege. As a matter of fact, his tours in Siberia were undertaken at the suggestion of the head of the Prisons Department in St. Petersburg, as his correspondence proves. Since Dr. Baedeker's retirement, the visitation of the prisons has been carried on by his true comrades in service, Baron Nicolai and Mr. Kargel. The "Englishman" appears to be a compound of a philanthropist-evangelist intent on doing good, and a newspaper-correspondent on the look-out for good "copy." He is ever making notes with a view to publication.

"'Let him see the prison in its glory,' said the General, the governor of the district. 'I have written about it, but they pay no attention to me. Let them find out from the foreign press!'"

The "Englishman" was a sightseer also. He had been to view the cathedral in this Siberian city, and the factory, and would not like to miss the prison. To him it was one of the show-places.

He apparently enjoyed his dinner at the General's table; "the handsome surroundings, the delicate dishes, the elegance and luxury of the house." The General's lady, who "held herself very erect, and kept her elbows close to her waist" was good company. He was full of talk about India. He begged his hostess to favour the company with a little music after dinner, and

> "with the ex-Director of a Department, she went to the grand piano (a splendid instrument), and they played in well-practised style Beethoven's Fifth Symphony."

Very good! But that is not Dr. Baedeker. He was no show-peeper. Far otherwise! From Constantinople he once wrote home:

> "Yesterday I visited the great Mosque of St. Sophia. But you know I am a bad hand at sight-seeing. It fatigues me much more than an entire day's preaching would. Of course, the building is grand and unique. The enormous dome, and the carvings and mosaics are wonderful and magnificent. To-day the Sultan was to enter it; but I feel no desire to be seen where there is no room for my Lord."

Tolstoy, with all his genius, has not surpassed that last sentence in the whole of his writings; and this, bear in mind, was never intended for the public eye!

> "How many prisoners are there in the cells? How many men? How many women? Children? Sick persons? Exiles? inquired the Englishman of the Inspector."

Yes! These are Dr. Baedeker's invariable questions. But it was neither coarse curiosity, nor "with a view to publication," that led him to ask them. They were generally put on a preliminary visit to the prisons, in order that he might know what quantity of Scriptures he would require when he went to preach the gospel. Experience had taught him that to avoid the trouble of carrying an unnecessary load of heavy books, or the annoyance and disappointment of running short, the simplest plan was to go first and find out how many people were confined in the place. How obvious it looks when it is explained! But it is when we come to Tolstoy's version of Baedeker's gospel that we find the novelist most at sea. Let us give Tolstoy the benefit of the doubt. He misrepresented because he did not comprehend. The "Englishman" is addressing the men through an interpreter.

> "'Tell them,' he said, 'that Christ loved them, and pitied them, and died for them. If they believe in this, they will be saved.'
> "While he spoke, all the prisoners stood silent, with their arms at their sides."

If the beloved preacher himself had had the revising of this report of his address, we know exactly how he would have altered it. As it stands, it is merely a dead creed, a record of events long past. Dr. Baedeker's message was something alive, full of power, full of love, a thing of the present instant.

"Tell them that Christ loves them *now*, and pities them *now*; that He once died for them, and *now lives* to help and bless them. If they believe in this, they cannot but be saved. Faith in Him will make new men of them."

A trifling alteration, but a very different message this, from Tolstoy's. A very slight touch by an expert watchmaker will make all the difference between a useless encumbrance and a reliable timekeeper. Tolstoy's watch is no good. The Count was clearly unable to grasp the vital essential of evangelical truth.

No fault need be found with his picture of the doctor's circulation of the New Testaments in the kameras. It is a vivid and pathetic scene.

"The Englishman took several bound Testaments out of a hand-bag, and many strong hands, with their hard black nails, stretched out towards him from beneath the coarse shirt-sleeves, jostling one another.

"The same thing happened in the second ward. There was the same foul air, the same icon hanging between the windows, the same tub to the left of the door; the prisoners were all lying side by side close to one another on the bed-shelves, and jumped up in the same manner and stood erect with their arms by their sides—all but three, who were ill.

'Tell them,' said the Englishman to the interpreter, 'that this Book will tell them all about it. Can any of them read?'

Count Tolstoy's "Englishman" is exhausted long before many of the cells have been visited.

"The depressing sights, and especially the stifling atmosphere, quelled even his energy."

Again, Tolstoy is hopelessly at variance with fact. We must pardon a novelist, however, in this. He is proceeding according to the probabilities of ordinary human nature. True, the average man would have had enough of it when he had inspected half a dozen of these fœtid hell-holes his energy would be "quelled."

But what kept Dr. Baedeker at it incessantly for fifteen years and more? What made him write from Tiflis:

"Visiting the prisons, and ministering to the poor souls who are under the awful power of sin and darkness, is indeed to me better than angel's food!"

Or this, the account of a Christmas day's work of love:

> "My interpreter and companion was taken ill with fever, and I went alone, and stumbled through a prison full of men, with the little help I found from a German prisoner."

Why did he not make the illness of his interpreter an excuse for remaining indoors that day? The answer is found in Jeremiah 20:9. If you are a Bible-reader, look at the verse; if not, you will never understand Dr. Baedeker, any more than Count Tolstoy understood him.

Mr. R. C. Morgan, whose tour with Dr. Baedeker among the prisons of Southern Russia in 1901 I have already referred to, described vividly at the time the unquenchable enthusiasm and untiring persistency of the doctor's prison visitations;

> "Think," said he, "of the labour of walking through a large building, giving several addresses, sometimes in very warm weather, with sympathies at extreme tension, drawn out by the ruined lives and darkened souls of the depressed and often hopeless prisoners, and testing everyone who claimed that he could read. I have been more than once wearied out in accompanying him; but the love he bears them, and the power of the gospel, and the joy of the Lord, are his strength."

Nor is there reason to complain of the results of the circulation of the New Testaments in the prison-houses, according to the novelist. For his novel concludes with long extracts from a gospel presented by the "Englishman," and with earnest moral reflections, excellent so far as they go, but hopelessly inadequate, deduced therefrom.

It is so very easy for Tolstoy to say what men *ought* to do, and what they *ought* to be; but Dr. Baedeker went forth to show even to the most degraded and destitute the Divine power that is at their service to lift them up into hope and worthiness and joy, the power of the living, loving Christ of God. St. Paul gets at the root of the matter when he says, *"If there had been a law given which could have given* Life, *verily righteousness should have been by the law"* (Galatians 3: 21). But law never did, and never will, convey the power to obey it. Nor was it simply a pretty theory that the doctor proclaimed; but a fact, demonstrated in countless instances, that He is able to save to the uttermost. He did not mock the prisoners, nor did they hear him unmoved, "silent, with their arms at their sides." This narrative lets us see how the poor thirsty souls drank eagerly of the living water. The full results we shall know in the light of Eternity.

The doctor used to tell of a conversation he had with Count Tolstoy in Moscow, in which the Count ought to have learned something about evangelical religion. The novelist, coarsely clad, received Dr. Baedeker in his plain and scantily furnished apartment. The two men sat and chatted together of England, and of contemporary Russian affairs.

What is your errand to Russia?" inquired the Count.

"To preach the gospel of Christ in the Russian prisons," he replied.

"There ought not to be any prisons!" exclaimed the novelist.

"So long as there is sin in the world there will be prisons," was the quiet rejoinder of the evangelist.

"There ought not to be sin in the world."

"What do you mean?"

"I mean that if people were properly taught, sin would not be!" said Tolstoy, with fiery emphasis.

For answer Dr. Baedeker quoted Luke 11:21 and 22: "When a strong man armed keepeth his palace, his goods are in peace. But when a stronger than he shall come upon him, and overcome him, he taketh from him all his armour wherein he trusted, and divideth his spoils."

"That is a parable of the soul of man and the devil's mastery over it," said the doctor. "That accounts for sin."

"Where is that?" inquired the Count, greatly interested.

"In Holy Scripture," he replied. "There is a stronger than we—the Evil One—against whom our natural armour of resolution and of moral codes, is useless. My message to the prisoners of Russia, and to all sinners everywhere, is, that there is a still Stronger One, Who is able to deliver the captives and slaves of Satan, and to transform them into the holy and beloved children of the Eternal and Holy God."

CHAPTER XVII

Weston-super-Mare, and Home

THE exigencies of space compel that this chapter shall be very brief.

When you walk along the promenade at Weston-super-Mare on a lovely summer day, and look out to sea, away beyond the islet called Steep Holme, five miles from the beach—the only permanent object above the water between yourself and New York—think of Dr. Baedeker. His home nestled on the beautiful hillside under the wood, between the great quarry and a long red-roofed church, both of which you can plainly see from the promenade. Through the leafy treetops of Grove Park you may obtain from its windows charming views of the bay; and of , yonder great headland, Brean Down; and glimpses of the far-stretching Bridgwater Bay beyond. On the sands close to the parade he was a familiar figure on summer Sunday evenings, when to great crowds of holiday-makers he preached the grand old gospel, whose power to save to the uttermost he had so often proved. He usually stood with a company of brethren like-minded, near the central pier—there was no pier there in those days—in that part of the beach on which on week-days the masses of the people make high holiday after their familiar seaside manner.

The residence of the doctor was named *Wart Eck,* which means "Waiting Corner." He and his wife spent their consecrated lives "looking for that blessed hope and the glorious appearing," and so they happily abode at "Waiting Corner!"

The three British institutions into whose operations he threw himself with intensity, whenever he was in this country, were the *British and Foreign Bible Society,* the *Evangelical Alliance,* and the *Protestant Alliance.* The British and Foreign Bible Society gave valuable help to Dr. Baedeker by supplying him at greatly reduced rates year after year with many thousands of New Testaments and other Scripture portions, for free circulation in the prisons. The doctor always gratefully acknowledged his indebtedness to the Society, zealously advocated its claims on many platforms at home and in foreign lands, and without doubt strengthened the hands of many of its agents in the localities visited by him. An examination of his letters home, frequently reveals an almost painful economy in his travelling, hotel, and other personal expenses, in order that he might devote his means to the uttermost, in providing the amounts necessary to purchase supplies of the Word of God on the favourable terms offered by the Society. The Evangelical Alliance found in him a vigorous representative—particularly in the Annual Week of Prayer, the arrangements for which, in Weston-super-Mare, for some years he controlled. Oh, how easily and irresistibly he led us before the throne, when he arose and broke forth into utterances of adoration and worship! The Protestant Alliance and the Reformation Society were upheld in a meeting for prayer held monthly in his drawing-room. He was generally absent, serving the Lord abroad; but we never forgot to pray for our dear host at such times.

The three figures at the gateway entrance to *Wart Eck* in the picture are the doctor and Mrs. Baedeker, and Mrs. Murray (now missionary in Chifu, China), their adopted daughter—the "Emmie" so fondly spoken of in his Siberian letters. Emmie was married to a Scotch missionary in the year 1891, the doctor calling at Chifu on his way

Weston-super-Mare
Photograph by Mr. W. A. Huntley

Dr. Baedeker's Residence, Weston-Super-Mare
Photograph by Mr. Hopwood

home from Siberia, after his second journey across Asia, in order to unite the young couple.

When in Weston, Dr. Baedeker regularly attended the Lord's Day meetings in the Gospel Hall, Waterloo Street, throwing himself with the utmost heartiness into the simple fellowship and worship of that assembly of devout believers. His sympathies were wide and strong; and his venerable figure was familiar and ever welcome in all meetings of his fellow-Christians that he was able to attend in the town.

His Weston friends cherish a bright memory of him singing, with evident enjoyment and enthusiasm, the familiar verse, so descriptive of his own life—

> "There are lonely hearts to cherish,
>   While the days are going by."

The last letter from abroad, in the selection in my hands, tells of meetings in Dresden; in "beloved Bohemia, beginning in Prague, the martyr-city of Huss"; in Vienna; and in Buda-

> SCRIPTURE TESTIMONY
>
> *There is no sting in death for the believer*
>
> I CORINTHIANS 15:54-57

Pesth. Evidently it was written with a trembling hand; but it flowed from a heart as great and as warm as ever. It closes significantly:

"Much love to all the saints.

> "'The sands of time are sinking,
>   The dawn of heaven breaks.'"

These words I transcribe in a dim twilight, in which I am scarcely able to distinguish my writing. How different his condition! He is in the full splendour of the glory of his Lord. The dawn has come, and the shadows have departed for ever. His home-call came when attending a conference at Clifton, Bristol. A chill developed into pneumonia; and he passed away after a few days' illness, in joy and triumph. During those few days the one sentence continually upon his lips was:

"I am going in to see the King in His beauty!"

He who had on earth sat familiarly with princes and nobles, and who had preached the gospel in the private apartments of monarchs, was at last on the threshold of his most privileged and sublime interview. The death-chamber was the ante-room of heaven. Those who entered it with hushed footstep were awed and stirred by influences unseen and realities eternal. Oh, it was a grand homegoing! The death, like the life, was magnificent.

It was so very appropriate that, in the good providence of God, Lord Radstock was in England, and able to be present at the funeral. His lordship recalled, in his addresses on the occasion, the striking circumstances of the doctor's conversion, and of his introduction to his vast life-work. It was also peculiarly appropriate that the only wreath that (at the request of Mrs. Baedeker) was permitted to lie upon the newly closed grave, was the lovely expression of the heartfelt sorrow of his grateful friends in Russia, brought post-haste from London, just in time for the last solemn ceremonies.

His mortal remains lie at rest, awaiting the glory of the resurrection morning, on the gentle slope of the Weston hill that faces south, for he ever loved the sunshine. Above, rise the wood-crowned heights; away below, the sea in Weston Bay ceaselessly ebbs and flows upon the wide sands; beyond, are headlands and hills—the Mendips and the Quantocks—a panorama of peace and beauty. His grave is near to that of his old and valued friend, the eighth Earl of Cavan; and is about half a mile from the dear Waiting Corner in which he abode— at intervals—for many years, looking for that blessed hope; and to which when travelling afar, in strange scenes and in remote corners of Europe and Asia, his heart so yearningly turned.

On the headstone of his grave Mrs. Baedeker has had engraven this inscription:

Friedrich Wilhelm Baedeker, Ph.D.
Went in to see the King in His Beauty,
Saved by the Precious Blood of the Lord Jesus,
October 9th, 1906.
Aged 83 years.

CHAPTER XVIII

The Prophet cries aloud

L ET us listen to the penetrating, burning, sentences addressed to us by this servant of God, now in his Master's immediate presence. He being dead, yet speaketh.

I. On Surfeit at Home, and Starvation Abroad

From Saratov, Russia.—"Thousands in the little island in the Northern Sea, called Great Britain, have been feasting on fat things, each feasting on the great fulness that is in Christ, leaving that fulness undiminished; but have you looked at the map of the world? What right have we to monopolise God's gift of the gospel, and let the multitude starve?

"Light is intended to shine in darkness. If brethren in England knew what I know, they would go to the ends of the earth to take light to those dark places."

From Sevastopol.—"Maps are very useful. Place them in the assemblies of the saints to remind them of the unpaid debt we owe to the nations of the earth."

From the banks of the river Ural.—"These nations and peoples are like sheep without a shepherd. What has the Church of God been about these eighteen hundred years? How is it possible that Lord's day after Lord's day, brethren and sisters feast at home, and have nothing to send to those for whom nothing is prepared? Oh, how I wish that the godly young men and women of Britain had but a glimpse of the utter neglect of these Asiatic races!

"Was Paul the *only* debtor to the Greeks and to the Barbarians? Are we now merely to comfort ourselves by admiring his burning zeal? A few loving words would do more here, would do more good than many excellent gospel addresses do in our comfortable buildings at home. How much owest *thou* unto my Lord?

"I am getting old, and my time is running out; but looking over the vast fields, I feel as if three lives were springing up within me, striving to be spent in the noble service of my blessed Lord.

"Does God care any more for a high-bred Englishman than for any one of these Asiatics? The precious food that is trodden underfoot on a single Lord's day in England, would be sufficient to save a whole heathen nation from starvation. Sin is abounding where is the grace of God yet more abounding? Has our gospel been polished down, to a beautiful set of doctrines, admired by saints at home, while sinners are going to hell without a warning given?"

From Odessa.—"With all the good things, and the fat things at home, the question comes to me again and again, *Cui bono?* What about the waste, howling wildernesses? *Are the little dogs feeding* even on the crumbs that fall from the master's table? I have just travelled through a country sunk in iniquity; and there is scarcely any witness for Truth.... There are here a great many

English steamers lading wheat; but no one seems to care for the souls of the sailors in them."

From Orenburg.—"'England has no need of me. There are too many preachers and teachers there. The living water does not flow out, and therefore it becomes stagnant. Here are vast fields of unevangelised peoples. There is a large bazaar some short distance from here on the Siberian side where a great trade is carried on. There are Bokharans, Tartars, Kalmucks, Kirghese, etc., merchants with their bales of goods, camels ready for transit. Walking across the Ural bridge is out of Europe into Asia; and the vast Asiatic steppe stretches before us to the horizon. Time is rapidly passing on. Oh that men might be ready and willing to do the work of an evangelist in such places as this, instead of splitting hairs in religious discussion in England, for which no one is any the better. It is more and more in my heart to send portions to those for whom nothing is prepared."

From Zurich.—"I am more and more convinced that there are too many Christians in one place in England; and that very many of them might be spared to serve the Lord in other lands."

From Prague.—"I have just returned from the last meeting. It has been a full and fruitful day; souls have been born for eternal life. The dear, dear Czechs! It is a great joy, and a feast of fat things, to be allowed to feed hungry souls."

From Berlin.—"There are many, many open doors for the glorious gospel; and you will not misunderstand me if I say there seems to be much waste in preaching to people who have known it many, many years, and withholding it from the hunger-ing, needy souls. I am thankful for every labourer in the various fields. Praise God for every soul conquered by the Lord—old and young, rich and poor. I am thankful for every remembrance in prayer, for every token of sympathy in the various members of the Body of Christ. Still the prayer for more labourers to be sent forth is laid upon us by the Lord of the harvest. Is not the whole Church sent into the world, even as the Lord Himself was sent into the world? See John 17:18, and 20:21.

> "'Oh for a thousand tongues to sing
> My great Redeemer's praise!'

What a reckoning there will be of debts not paid by Christians!"

From Bukharest.—What a blessing it is that in the Body of Christ there are poor and suffering members as well as strong and rich ones! How high and dry and barren we should be, but for the needy ones who claim our sympathy and our help. 'Those members of the body which seem to be more feeble, are necessary.' I am to see the Queen of Roumania to-day, and hope she may allow me to visit the prisons and the barracks. This is a very worldly, gay city; ...but there are nuggets of pure gold and precious jewels that have to be sought out. A number of poor Armenian refugees are here also, who lay claim to one's sympathy. We had a very happy three days' conference at Constanta with brethren of different nations and denominations. There were 'waters to swim in.' He is good!

"Oh that the various gifts in the Body of Christ were brought into active flow! There is no lack, but there is stagnation. There is too much waste in spending on one's self. 'He died for all, that they who live should not live to themselves, but unto Him!' There is a church-self and a national-self, as well as a personal and a family self. Apply the 'not' to them all."

From Helsingfors.—"The Shout of a king is in the camp! My body is the Master's, for His service! He gives strength sufficient. Last night and this morning the trumpet gave a clear sound.... I look to the Lord for a real reaping-time for Him. The one hundred and fifty-three fishes for the Resurrection Net are not all inside yet. They will have to be there before the net will be drawn to land, and the Master sits down with His servants.

"Last night I preached in the Chemical Laboratory of the University in German; this morning in the Methodist Hall, by interpretation into Swedish; at five this afternoon at Miss Sahiberg's, by interpretation from English into Swedish; and this evening by interpretation from German into Swedish in a large hall where we were once together on a Sunday; to-morrow I am asked to visit a Home for poor fallen girls, and afterwards to visit the German Girls' School. Many of the University students have decided for Christ at the meetings.

"There was a very crowded meeting. The Lord gave the Word with power. It cut right and left; but also the Healing Hand was manifest. This evening I speak once more at the University Laboratory,

"Let us not shut up our bowels of compassion. 'Give ye them to eat!'"

From Hattingen.—"It is always a trial of faith to me to begin in a new, strange place; yet the Lord has been so good, that I dare not fear."

From Sevastopol.—"'Oh that my head were waters, and mine eyes a fountain of tears, that I might weep' over these poor chained and unchained criminals! One can do so little for them; and yet a ray of light may be thrown into many a darkened life. If we knew more about them, we should pray more for the prisoners;

and also for the keepers of prisons. Many of the latter have given me a warm reception. I have had the joy of speaking to them of the great Redemption and of the Lord, and we have parted as brethren. May the Lord make the testimony fruitful for eternity!"

II. On the Necessity of Conscience of Sin

From Abo, Finland.—"Our meetings have been greatly blessed. Last night I spoke on Sin; showing the need of a Sin-bearer. I believe if sin were more fully recognised, people would not dispute so much about views and opinions, but they would fly for refuge from the wrath to come. Sin assumes such subtle disguises that people know but little of it; underneath, however, it is horrible, demoniacal. It is so easy to say, parrot-like, 'All have sinned, and come short of the glory of God.' Does it not seem a mockery, when the awful tyranny of sin is enslaving them, that people should hold a costly and beautiful prayer-book in their hands, and say, 'We are miserable offenders;' 'there is no health in us!' How can they hold the book? How can they stand upright? How can they intone the words, setting them to pleasant music? There is something so utterly wrong in our forms of religion when they are divorced from the power.

"This is a fine city; and just now in its winter garb of white, with a glorious sun shining upon it, it looks very bright. But they say the summer is the time to see the beauties of the country. However, I don't wish to admire scenery, when the Devil is holding men's souls so tightly in his grasp, because they know not Him who is able and waiting to deliver them. Oh, what a debt we owe! At 10:30 this morning I have a meeting in English-Swedish; this evening at 6:30, in English-Finnish. God bless you, my darling, and keep you with your face anointed, and your heart bounding with joy, because you are allowed to deny yourself for His Name's and the glorious Gospel's sake!"

From Cassel.—"Call sinners by their real names, or they will never become Christians I"

From Buda-Pesth.—"It is a sad pity that in the prayers of God's children, and in their evangelising efforts, so little is thought of these vast regions containing many millions of heathen who bear the name of Christians, but who are under the power of darkness."

Extract from an address by the doctor in England.—"Near the frontier of the Austrian Empire, at Willzka, there is a deep salt-mine in which a number of men and women are employed. They work there from the beginning to the end of the year. In fact, they and their families live in that salt-mine. It is an underground village. Children are born and go to school in the mine, and they have a church there. They live and die in that salt-mine. The only sun they have is an artificial light. If it happens that one is brought up to the surface to see the dazzling light of the real sun, and to feel his warmth, he would naturally most reluctantly return to his former darkness. But there are those who live in a blacker darkness, upon whom the light of the Gospel of Christ never shines. What about them? Shall we allow them to remain slaves in their desperate mine? Surely the blackest darkness is not too dark for the beams of God's grace to lighten it!"

III. On the Only Hope

From Wesel.—"Last evening I had a meeting, with a very full attendance. My subject was 'Redemption through His Blood.'"

From Riga.—"Last night the hall was crammed full, and the Lord gave the word in the power and demonstration of the Holy Ghost. It will be a day not easily forgotten by many. The Lamb had all the glory!"

From the Black Sea.—"We steam along the coast of the Krimea, and have already stopped at Yalta and Feodosia. At the latter place Prince. G. and his wife landed with their servants. I had a good, and I trust profitable, conversation with the prince last night. He is a pleasant, intelligent man; and I had an opportunity to put the truth before him. The Lord carries this ship in the hollow of His hand. There are many Turks, Armenians, Tartars, and Germans on board; so I have precious opportunities of speaking a word for the Master.

"An Armenian did a kind act to a poor man of his nation, who had no ticket and was to be turned away from the ship. He paid the fare for him. This gave me an opportunity to speak to him. Telling him what Jesus had done for us, his heart responded warmly, and I believe he is a Christian. Of course, speaking to one, there are always many curious listeners. On board these steamers is a wonderful field for evangelising, with the constant change of passengers. 'Cast thy bread upon the waters, and thou shalt find it.'"

From Revel, Esthonia.—"The Greeks, and Lutherans, and Romans have shifted God's ancient landmark; putting ceremonies and sacraments, instead of the Blood."

Extract from an address delivered by the doctor in England.—"I once met a Tartar, a Mohammedan, who addressed the usual question to me:

"'What do you think of the prophet Mohammed?'

"'I have a much more important question for you, than that,' I said.

"'More important!' he exclaimed. 'What is it, then?'

"'It is, What do you think about Sin?'

"'Oh, we are all sinners,' he replied. He might have been an Englishman, so glibly did he say it.

"'Then you are a sinner, too?' I asked.

"'Yes, certainly.'

"'Can one sinner save another sinner?' said I.

"'No.'

"'But if he is a prophet?'

"'No.'

"'Well, then, what are we to do—all sinners?'

"He had no answer to that question; and I told him of One who knew no sin, Who was made sin for us. The Tartar bowed down his head, and his eyes filled with tears. He had never before heard the Sound of the gospel. He was only one of the millions of these men, fine men, beautiful in stature, walking like giants or kings, but enslaved by sin, and with no one to tell them of Him whose blood can set them free.

> **SCRIPTURE TESTIMONY**
>
> *Jesus became sin on our behalf, that we might become righteousness*
>
> 2 CORINTHIANS 5:11-17 · 2 CORINTHIANS 5:16-6:2 · EPHESIANS 2:13-19 · COLOSSIANS 1:20-23

"There is no power on earth that can save sinners from the Satanic power that holds them in its deadly grasp, except the power of the Lord Jesus Christ, the One who died and rose again. I long to go back to tell the people in these dark, dark regions of this wonderful love—the love of God in Christ Jesus. That is the story worth telling! And they listen to it! And oh, if they only knew it, they would not be the sinners that they are....

"The men have embraced me and kissed me, so glad were they for the message I was able to give them. If you have a real sinner before you, much eloquence is not needed, nor a long sermon."

On board steamer on a Siberian river.—"The sight of 5000 men in chains may move us to tears of pity, but what will tears avail? 'Nothing but the blood of Jesus' avails. It would be utter waste of breath and energy to try and do anything for this wreckage of humanity but preach to them 'Christ and Him crucified.' How eagerly they listened! No self-righteous excuses; no mocking now; all in the same condemnation."

From Helsingfors.—"What the people here want is, a living Christ!"

IV. On the Authority and Dignity of the Gospel

"My days are fully occupied in happy joyful service. I need the Master's presence and blessing day by day, and a message on every occasion from Himself. To-day I am to see the Princess Royal, and to give her a message from the King of kings.

"The message alone is not sufficient, if the messenger is not divinely authorised and especially sent. I want the fellowship of God's saints in this work; and I trust that many may be led to ask for me a fresh anointing with the HOLY GHOST."

Scripture Testimony Index

Faith and love are demonstrated by giving of oneself for others.. 2
1 John 3:16-18

Dr. Baedeker had a reputation for being a man who loved others; and was compared to the Apostle John, who wrote so much about love. Baedeker often left home with a rug, but he seldom returned with it, for nearly every time he had given it to someone he met on his travels who was in need.

Salvation transforms.. 17
2 Corinthians 5:16-17 · Galatians 6:15

Unbelieving, worldly, middle-aged Dr. Baedeker had reluctantly agreed to attend a series of Lord Radstock's evangelistic meetings. Baedeker would hurriedly leave after each service. But one evening the crowd prevented his quick escape, and so Lord Radstock was able to tell Dr. Baedeker that God had a message for him. Later Baedeker said about that meeting, "I went in a proud German infidel, and came out a humble, believing disciple of the Lord Jesus Christ." And the rest of Baedeker's life testified to his total transformation.

According to your faith be it done to you
Matthew 9:27-31

Acts 3:6 · Acts 3:16 · Acts 4:10 · Acts 4:30

Dr. Baedeker had always been in delicate health. But after his conversion, he stepped out in faith, abandoned his medication, and trusted God for his wellbeing. For the next forty years, as he dedicated his life to serving Christ, he enjoyed good health and vigor.

God's work will not lack God's supply
Philippians 4:19

Acts 10:19-20 · Acts 11:12

After Fraulein Blücher's conversion, she dedicated her life and resources to Kingdom service and opened a mission center, which soon became too small. The need for a bigger space brought her and her friends to God in prayer. While they were still praying, God sent a stranger to help meet the need.

Individuals opposed to the Gospel
Acts 8:3 · Acts 9:1-2

1 Peter 4:12-19

Colonel Paschkoff, an influential and wealthy officer of the Imperial Guards of Russia, was a devoted follower of Jesus. For his persistence in evangelizing, in holding prayer meetings and Bible studies, and for tract distribution, he was forever banished from Russia by Emperor Alexander III.

The righteous innately have God's heart toward those

Matthew 25:31-46

"I was in prison and you came to me." In the parable of the Sheep and the Goats in Matthew 25, Jesus provided examples of the kinds of things that a believer will do when his or her heart is aligned to the heart of God. In answer to prayer, Dr. Baedeker was given a permit to visit any prison in Russia, so that he could see those "who are kept out of sight, and are never thought of by others."

God is able to bring good from any circumstances 39
Romans 8:28

Once while jostling in a crowd of passengers trying to secure seats on the train to Moscow, Dr. Baedeker's pocket-book was stolen. Not only did it contain a considerable amount of money and his passport, but it had also contained his precious prisons-permit, without which he could not gain access to the prisons. But "God turned the curse into a blessing," in that the replacement prisons-permit granted even greater liberties and privileges.

As we serve Him, the Lord will be our defense 43
Luke 10:19 · 2 Thessalonians 3:1-3

When asked if her husband carried a weapon for protection given the places he went and the kinds of people he encountered in the course of his ministry, Mrs. Baedeker simply replied that he would never dream of arming himself. She was then asked, "Do you mean to say he went forth absolutely defenseless?" to which she replied, "By no means. God was his defense!"

As we serve Him, the Lord will be our defense 44
Luke 10:19 · 2 Thessalonians 3:1-3

Dr. Baedeker was told of a certain district where the men were wild, desperate and murderous; killing and robbing people of their possessions. His remarkable response to this forewarning was, "Tell me all about them, I mean to go there. Those people terribly need the gospel!" Baedeker went in spite of the risk and accomplished his mission unharmed.

Acts 9:23-25

Dr. Baedeker was preaching on the subject of "The Bible" in Zurich, which was like issuing a challenge to skeptical university students. The unbelievers attended in order to deride and to mock, and an excited mob gathered outside the hall shouting, "We will fling him into the lake when he comes out!" But like the Apostle Paul's escape through an opening in the wall, Dr. Baedeker was able to safely slip out the back.

Luke 18:7 · John 15:7 · Acts 12:5 · James 5:15

Dr. Baedeker's guide became very agitated after they found themselves lost in the middle of nowhere, in the winter, with nightfall fast approaching. Dr. Baedeker's immediate solution was to pray, while his guide would only fret. Finally, they knelt down together to pray, and their rescue came before they had even finished.

Luke 18:7 · John 15:7 · Acts 12:5 · James 5:15

A young man had been riding in a remote region, with not a house or human being as far as he could see, when the horse stumbled. This fellow, who was far from God in his heart, was thrown and broke his leg, and worse still, the horse ran away. Facing death by wolves or exposure, he cried out, "O God, if there be a God...have mercy..." and was promptly delivered in body and soul.

Deliverance from enemies and circumstances
Luke 1:71

Luke 22:43 · Acts 12:6-11

During a massacre of Armenians in Baku, mobs moved house to house, burning them and their occupants to ashes. Patwakan Tarajantz, Dr. Baedeker's ministry companion and interpreter, was at home with his wife and ten children. Faced with what seemed like inevitable death, Patwakan turned to God in prayer. Just as the mob reached his home God sent an unexpected deliverer, and the family was spared.

Do good to those who hate you..55
Matthew 5:44 · Luke 6:27

Patwakan Tarajantz and his family were miraculously spared a fiery death at the hands of angry mobs of those who hated the Armenians. In a demonstration of "do good to those who hate you," and with the help of the British and Foreign Bible Society, Mr. Tarajantz supplied the bread of everlasting life to his would-be murderers.

As we serve Him, the Lord will be our defense........................55
Luke 10:19 · 2 Thessalonians 3:1-3

Dr. Baedeker forgot his host's warning about a vicious guard dog, walked out into the yard, and roused the beast. In trying to run away, he stumbled and fell hard, while the dog came rushing up, growling angrily. Dr. Baedeker's heart went to heaven in a prayer for protection. Just as God shut the mouths of the lions for Daniel, to everyone's surprise, the dog merely sniffed, then went back to his kennel.

God gives wisdom to work even within dishonest situations...57
Luke 16:1-9

When the police in Riga would not allow Dr. Baedeker to go ahead with a planned meeting because preaching by "unauthorized persons" was prohibited, he shrewdly found a loophole in the law and took advantage of it to share the gospel over several nights to thousands of people in the city.

The willingness of the Esthonians to hear the gospel notwithstanding, Dr. Baedeker was faced with strong opposition from Lutheran priests who believed only workers ordained by them should share the gospel. They went out of their way in an attempt to block him, eventually sending the police.

Dr. Baedeker exemplified the parable of the talents in which Jesus describes faithful servants as those who invest one hundred percent of what the Master had entrusted to them. Baedeker was a successful man, and after his conversion, he used all of his time and resources to increase the Master's Kingdom.

Dr. Baedeker presented a convicted murderer who could not read with a "Wordless Book," and took the time to lovingly walk the fellow through its three leaves and their meanings. At the end of his visit, the grateful prisoner tearfully declared, "Thank you, sir, a thousandfold, for bringing such a message to such an unworthy wretch as I am!"

Dr. Baedeker, filled with compassion, arranged to provide a proper, hearty meal for over five hundred emigrants and discharged soldiers—all poor and starving—who were aboard a ship with him. Dr. Baedeker found true joy as he watched the people enjoy the meal, looking to God in thanksgiving, and there were many opportunities to speak to them about spiritual matters.

Give to everyone who asks
*Matthew 5:42 · Luke 6:30 · Acts 20:35 · 2 Corinthians 8:1-2 ·
1 John 3:17*

The righteous innately have God's heart toward those in need .. 122
Matthew 25:31-46

A nobleman—now a wreck in piteous condition—had been banished and imprisoned in Siberia for some crime. When the poor man asked for help, Dr. Baedeker gave him money and clothes, which caused the grateful man to burst into a flood of tears.

A sower went out to sow seed, and some bore much fruit 132
Matthew 13:20-23 · Mark 4:3-9 · Mark 4:14-20 · Luke 8:4-15

Like "bread cast upon the waters" returning "after many days," Dr. Baedeker was encouraged to meet with a prisoner who had been blessed by his preaching many years before, and to hear about how he had grown in his faith since that time.

Jesus came for sinners and those rejected by society 151
Matthew 8:1-13 · Matthew 26:6 · Luke 5:30 · Luke 7:34

Baroness Mathilda von Wrede, who clearly had God's heart, was able to translate the warmth of Dr. Baedeker's Gospel sermon into Finnish. Previously a university professor had given a sterile translation. While the prisoners were unaffected by the professor's words, they were moved to tears when they heard Baedeker address them as "beloved friends," and "brothers."

Jesus will never send away those who come to Him 155
John 6:37

Baroness von Wrede was compelled by compassion for a particularly hard-hearted and dangerous criminal. At first, he was adamantly opposed to her, covering his ears, and threatening to kill her. But she prayed continually for him and visited him again and again, until eventually God broke his stony heart. With deep penitence he took his awful crimes to Him who said, "I will in no wise reject him that comes."

While traveling in Sweden, Dr. Baedeker gave a tract to an agnostic woman, lovingly challenging her to read it and to think about it. After more conversation, he gave her his card and asked her to promise to let him know when she had finally met Jesus. Eight years later, he got a letter. She had come to faith in Jesus!

Dr. Baedeker delighted in his missionary journeys in the Ararat vicinity, in spite of the difficulty of travel and tremendous risk to his life. All that mattered to him were the downtrodden in need of cheer, and the Christians to be nourished with the word of God.

"Our house belongs to the Lord Jesus. Therefore regard it as your dwelling-place whenever you come to Baku." These were the sweet words of Dr. Baedeker's Christian hosts, and so warm was their hospitality that he remarked, "We may teach them from the Word; but they act the Word, and leave us far behind."

A Stundist believer from Russia shared with Dr. Baedeker the great persecution his family had to endure because of their faith in Jesus; not from the government or State church but from a merciless mob of neighbors, and even more sadly, an enemy within; his own brother.

As the curtains drew on the life of Dr. Baedeker, his last moments were not spent in fear of death. Rather with joy he continued to declare, until his triumphant exit, "I AM GOING IN TO SEE THE KING IN HIS BEAUTY!"

Dr. Baedeker had a most interesting conversation with a Muslim. The man wanted to know what Baedeker thought about the prophet Mohammed. The doctor answered by asking another question about Sin, which led the Mohammedan to see the obvious need for the Savior, Jesus Christ.

Walking Together Press is a non-profit publishing company devoted to supporting grassroots libraries in Africa through global book sales and through providing free library editions.

To read our story, to see our catalog, and to learn more about how you can help us in our mission, visit our website at:

https://walkingtogether.press

www.ingramcontent.com/pod-product-compliance
Lightning Source LLC
Chambersburg PA
CBHW021130070726
47591CB00014B/2251